A BLOODY DAWN

Lieutenant Colonel Dan Harvey, now retired, served on operations at home and abroad for forty years, including tours of duty in the Middle East, Africa, the Balkans and South Caucasus, with the UN, EU, NATO PfP and OSCE. He is the author of *Soldiering against Subversion: The Irish Defence Forces and Internal Security During the Troubles, 1969–1998* (2018); *Into Action: Irish Peacekeepers Under Fire, 1960–2014* (2017); *A Bloody Day: The Irish at Waterloo* and *A Bloody Night: The Irish at Rorke's Drift* (both reissued 2017); and *Soldiers of the Short Grass: A History of the Curragh Camp* (2016).

IN THIS SERIES

A Bloody Day: The Irish at Waterloo (2017)

A Bloody Night: The Irish at Rorke's Drift (2017)

A Bloody Week: The Irish at Arnhem (2019)

A BLOODY DAWN

THE IRISH AT D-DAY

DAN HARVEY

MERRION
PRESS

First published in 2019 by
Merrion Press
An imprint of Irish Academic Press
10 George's Street
Newbridge
Co. Kildare
Ireland
www.merrionpress.ie

9781785372414 (Paper)
9781785372421 (Kindle)
9781785372438 (Epub)
9781785372445 (PDF)

British Library Cataloguing in Publication Data
An entry can be found on request

Library of Congress Cataloging in Publication Data
An entry can be found on request

Typeset in Bembo MT Std 11/15 pt

Cover front: American craft and personnel arrive at
Omaha Beach, Irish amongst them, 6 June 1944.
(World History Archive/Alamy Stock Photo)
Cover back: RAF Dakota, 6 June 1944.
(Gary Eason/Flight Artworks/Alamy Stock Photo)

CONTENTS

Allied Breakout Plan
Battle of Normandy

British 2nd Army with Canadian 1st Army 'Fix' and attract Germans drawing in their reserves especially their tanks. U.S. 1st and 3rd Armies with far less dense opposition, especially tanks, 'Break-out' southwards, then swing east.

D-Day Assault Invasion Plan
Normandy

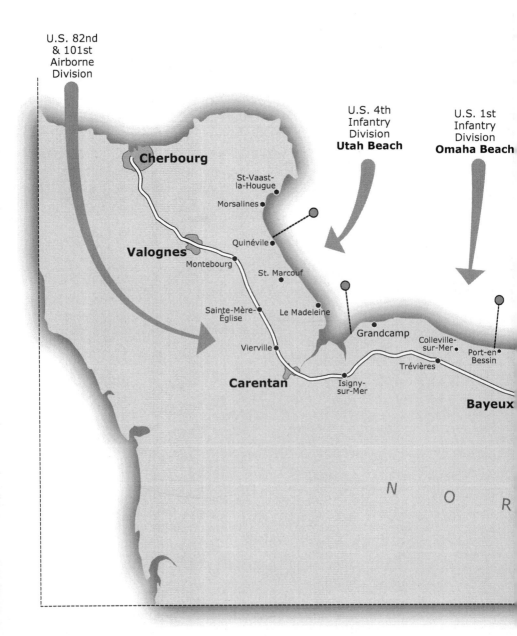

U.S. 82nd
& 101st
Airborne
Division

U.S. 4th
Infantry
Division
Utah Beach

U.S. 1st
Infantry
Division
Omaha Beach

Cherbourg

St-Vaast-
la-Hougue

Morsalines

Quinévile

Valognes

Montebourg

St. Marcouf

Sainte-Mère-
Église

Le Madeleine

Vierville

Grandcamp

Colleville-
sur-Mer

Port-en
Bessin

Trévières

Carentan

Isigny-
sur-Mer

Bayeux

N O R

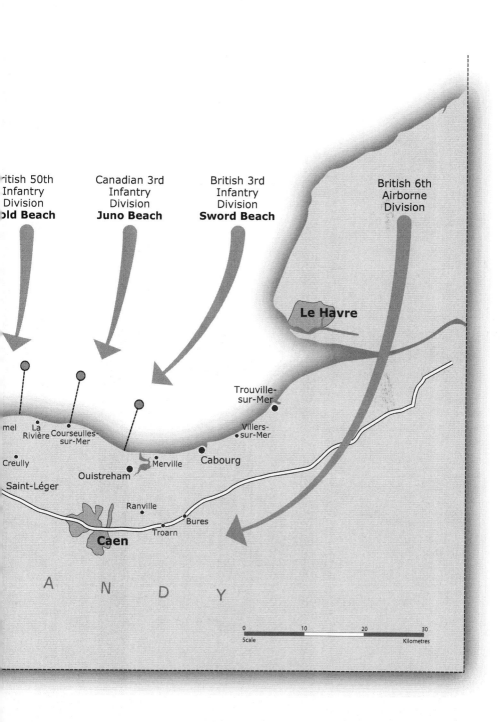

British 50th
Infantry
Division
old Beach

Canadian 3rd
Infantry
Division
Juno Beach

British 3rd
Infantry
Division
Sword Beach

British 6th
Airborne
Division

Le Havre

Trouville-
sur-Mer

Villers-
sur-Mer

mel
La
Rivière
Courseulles-
sur-Mer

Cabourg

Creully

Merville

Ouistreham

Saint-Léger

Ranville

Bures

Troarn

Caen

A   N   D   Y

0   10   20   30
Scale   Kilometres

The D-Day Landing

PHASE 1 **Airborne drop** Midnight–2AM *Over 13,000 paratroopers dropped behind enemy lines.*

PHASE 2 **Art of deceit** 1AM–4AM *The Allies faked another invasion in Pas de Calais.*

PHASE 3 **Aerial attack** 3AM *300 planes dropped 13,000 bombs on German defences.*

PHASE 4 **Naval attack** 5AM *Naval bombardment preceded the invasion.*

PHASE 5 **The invasion**

German batteries

Paratrooper drop zone

Areas captured by the Allies at midnight

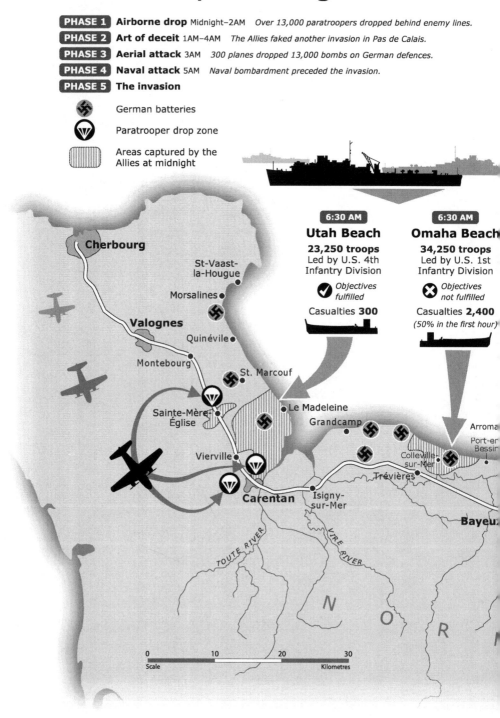

6:30 AM

Utah Beach

23,250 troops
Led by U.S. 4th
Infantry Division

✓ Objectives fulfilled

Casualties **300**

6:30 AM

Omaha Beach

34,250 troops
Led by U.S. 1st
Infantry Division

✗ Objectives not fulfilled

Casualties **2,400**
(50% in the first hour)

Cherbourg

St-Vaast-la-Hougue

Morsalines

Valognes

Quinéville

Montebourg

Sainte-Mère-Église

Vierville

Le Madeleine

Grandcamp

Arroma

Port-er Bessir

Colleville-sur-Mer

Trévières

Carentan Isigny-sur-Mer

St. Marcouf

Bayeu

TOUTE RIVER

VIRE RIVER

N O R N

0   10   20   30
Scale   Kilometres

6 June 1944

Supreme Commander
General Dwight D. Eisenhower

Soldiers: 156,000 troops
(73,000 U.S. Army, 83,000 British & Canadian)

Aircraft: 11,590

Navy: 6,939 vessels
(1,213 naval combat ships, 4,126 landing craft, 736 ancillary craft, 864 merchant vessels)
Navy personnel: 195,700 men
(52,889 U.S., 112,824 British, 4,988 other Allied countries)

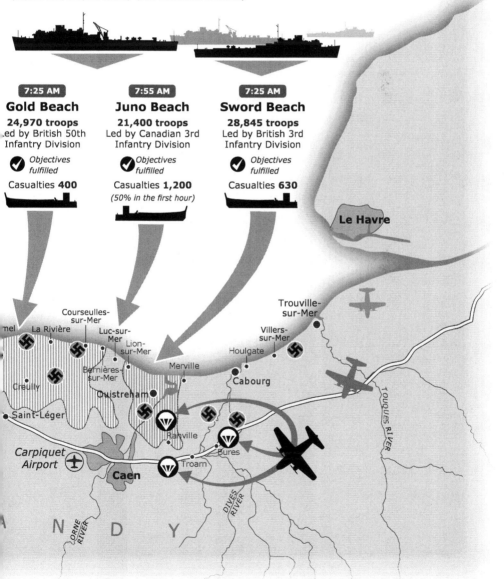

7:25 AM

Gold Beach

24,970 troops
_ed by British 50th
Infantry Division

✔ *Objectives
fulfilled*

Casualties **400**

7:55 AM

Juno Beach

21,400 troops
Led by Canadian 3rd
Infantry Division

✔ *Objectives
fulfilled*

Casualties **1,200**
(50% in the first hour)

7:25 AM

Sword Beach

28,845 troops
Led by British 3rd
Infantry Division

✔ *Objectives
fulfilled*

Casualties **630**

Le Havre

Trouville-
sur-Mer

Courseulles-
sur-Mer

nel La Rivière

Luc-sur-
Mer Lion-
sur-Mer

Villers-
sur-Mer

Houlgate

Créuly

Bernières-
sur-Mer

Merville

Cabourg

Saint-Léger

Ouistreham

Carpiquet
Airport

Ranville

Bures

Troarn

Caen

TOUQUES RIVER

DIVES RIVER

ORNE RIVER

A N D Y

ACKNOWLEDGEMENTS

When I was a boy growing up in Cork city throughout the 1960s and 1970s, the Second World War had not really been over for that long. When the neighbouring families required a babysitter I sometimes substituted for my older sister, and one evening in a nearby house, on just such an occasion, I found myself receiving a rather rushed 'babysitter briefing' from the mother concerned. In the background, a decidedly distracted and flustered husband was rummaging around in the drawers of a sideboard, seeking something critical for the evening ahead. While he was conducting his urgent search, he left one of the drawers sufficiently ajar that I could plainly see the outline of what was unmistakably a Hitler Youth knife, etched with the motto '*Blut und Ehre*' (Blood and Honour). It was an item instantly recognisable to a young teenage boy of the time, for the Nazis were still the villains in comics like *The Victor* and at the pictures, and that was what all young boys knew.

The much sought-after item found, the couple hurriedly departed, uncharacteristically leaving the sideboard drawers unlocked. Intrigued, excited, and fascinated all at once, I wondered how the knife came to be there. Had its current owner taken it as a war trophy during military service in the British Army, and was there a story attached to its coming into his possession? Opening the drawer gingerly, I dared take it out and hold it in my hands. I was captivated and my imagination took full flight, transporting me to a daring night-time commando raid, a clandestine parachute drop behind enemy lines, the situations and scenarios limitless. It was the shortest babysitting session I ever experienced, as I imagined commandos fighting hand-to-hand in a desperate life-or-death struggle against a ruthless Nazi enemy.

Acknowledgements

On the return of the couple from their evening out, I was acutely tempted to ask the husband about the story of the knife, but at that age I was not old enough to ask directly, and anyway it was not appropriate under the circumstances. I resolved to get to the bottom of the matter, but unfortunately the family left the neighbourhood shortly thereafter and moved to Dublin, and to this day my quest was unfulfilled. Ever mindful of this, I decided that if I was ever again faced with a similar situation of encountering a Second World War veteran, I would not let the occasion of such meetings go by without at least enquiring into their wartime experiences. And so it was, and although such encounters were infrequent, they were very informative. Since then I have read, researched and reflected on the topic at length, specifically on the D–Day battlefield, and I have visited its beaches and areas of interest around the Normandy shoreline. Conscious of there being no overall associated 'Irish narrative' as such, but knowing of individual involvements, I have always felt that only part was known of a larger, more complete and comprehensive participation of Irish forces, and so over time set about building up a story of the Irish contribution to the Normandy invasion.

In revealing this story of the 'D–Day Irish', I wish to acknowledge the advice and assistance of the staff of the Reference Section of the Imperial War Museum, London; Professor Jane Maxwell, Trinity College Dublin; Brenda Malone, National Museum of Ireland; Richard Bradfield, Boole Library, University College Cork; Professor Geoff Roberts, School of History, University College Cork; Doctor Steven O'Connor, Centre d'histoire de Sciences Po, Paris; Stephen Leach, Local History Department, Cork City Library; Sergeant Wayne Fitzgerald, Editor, *An Cosantóir* (the Irish Defence Forces magazine); Lieutenant-Colonel Fred O'Donovan, for information on his father and uncle; and Phillip Ness, for details about his father's D–Day participation.

I would also like to thank Kevin Myers for writing the Foreword to the book and otherwise for being in front of most everyone else in his consistent efforts over the decades to seek recognition for the involvement of Irish men and women in both World Wars, and to Richard Doherty, whose much-needed books on the 'Irish' involvement in the Second World War amply and authoritatively illustrate this fact. Both have been generous with their time, knowledge and wisdom, and indeed have displayed great courtesy and patience with me, thank you sincerely.

To Paul O'Flynn, for his immensely practical help with many matters associated with getting the manuscript and illustrations ready. To Deirdre Maxwell, for transforming my handwritten manuscript into a professionally typed, presentable version. Thereafter to Conor Graham, Publisher and Managing Director of Merrion Press, his Managing Editor, Fiona Dunne, Marketing Manager Maeve Convery, and editor Keith Devereux for seeing the book's production from concept through process to becoming a reality, and for their overall faith in the project.

FOREWORD

When 22-year-old Private Edward Delaney O'Sullivan of the 22nd Independent (Pathfinder) Company of the Parachute Regiment touched down outside the little Normandy village of Touffreville around 4 am, 6 June 1944, he was the human vanguard of one of the greatest military advances in world history. Up until he landed, almost the entire Eurasian landmass, from the North Cape of Norway to the South China Sea and from Cadiz in the Eastern Atlantic to the Sea of Okhots in the Western Pacific, with the exception of the Alpine ambiguities of Switzerland and the Nazi-affable, ore-suppling Nordic neutrality of Sweden, was under some kind of totalitarian rule.

For a brief while, the Irish-born O'Sullivan was the sole armed embodiment of freedom on the European mainland. His was not the individual liberty of the gallant resistance fighters, whose freedom was individual, existential and moral, but that of an entire culture, arriving under arms to displace the genocidal murderousness of the Third Reich. We cannot know what this brave Irishman felt about being the harbinger of freedom for France and for Europe, for he was soon to die in a brief and mutually fatal firefight with a German soldier. If ever a man deserved to be honoured in his native land, it is he.

In the month of June seventy-five years ago, at least 301 Irishmen were killed with British and Canadian forces in the war against the Third Reich – ten per day – even though most of the Irish regiments of foot, the Irish Guards, the Royal Inniskilling Fusiliers and the Royal Irish Fusiliers, were not seriously in action during that time. Sixty-eight Irishmen were killed with the Royal Ulster Rifles, the only regiment in the British Army to supply two battalions on D-Day. The rest of the 230 or so Irish dead were killed in a variety of other regiments, in which many had already distinguished themselves.

One in thirty of all warrant officers in the British Army to die during the war came from independent Ireland. In addition, over one hundred Irishmen were killed serving with the Parachute Regiment. 100 and thirty of the Special Air Service were killed in deep penetration raids behind enemy lines; 10 per cent of them were Irish. Indeed, an Irish soldier was nearly six times more likely to join the SAS than were his British equivalents. There was a price for this kind of daring. At least eleven Irishmen captured while serving with Special Forces were murdered by the Nazis. Such soldiers are mentioned here because, although outside the purview of this book, they serve to remind the reader of the huge contribution Irish volunteers made to the Allied cause – and never more so than by the men and the women mentioned in the pages that follow.

Colonel Dan Harvey is uniquely qualified to remind us of the Irish of D-Day, for he is a much-published author and a former officer in the Defence Forces. Furthermore, Normandy 1944 is the perfect place in which to take a snapshot of Irish participation in the war against the Third Reich. Because the War Office was reluctant to admit too many soldiers from independent Ireland into one regiment – even ones like the Irish Guards or the Inniskilling Fusiliers – which might then become more loyal to Dublin than London, Irish volunteers were dispersed throughout the British Army, Air Force and Navy. It is only when all those arms came together, as they did in June 1944, that we get a real picture of Irish involvement in a war that finally lifted Nazi tyranny from the peoples of Europe.

But let it be remembered, as Colonel Harvey reminds us here, that it was a vital weather report from 'neutral' Ireland, authorised by de Valera's government, which made possible the Normandy landings. The history of the world was changed by that absolutely vital piece of meteorological intelligence, confirming this unassailable truth: D-Day is in part a truly Irish story, which this book tells in all its thrilling and tragic detail.

Kevin Myers, May 2019

PREFACE

There had been other land invasions during the Second World War (North Africa, Sicily and Salerno among them) but D-Day 6 June 1944 was different. The Normandy landings were staggering in scope, and the history of warfare had never known a comparable amphibious invasion for its breath of conception, grandeur of scale and mastery of execution. Operation Overlord, the opening of the 'second front' against the German Army, was a bid to restore liberty to Nazi-occupied western Europe and laid the foundations of the Allied victory. This book is dedicated to the 'D-Day Irish', both native-born and of Irish descent, whose involvement on D-Day and in the Normandy Campaign must be acknowledged and not forgotten, and the values for which they fought must never be lost.

> The reality there was the chaos. It was not that you were terrified, it was that you did not know where the Germans were; you did not know where your comrades were. You could not walk very fast, weighed down with heavy equipment, and because of the bad weather the reinforcements that were meant to come at 0900 hours that morning, about six hours after we jumped, did not arrive until 3pm, at which stage the main battles were over and you were either, dead, wounded or exhausted.
>
> *Lieutenant Leonard Wrigley (Waterford),*
> *British 6th Airborne Division*

As I parachuted down, the noise became overwhelming – machine guns, shells and mortars. It was impossible to tell who anyone was. I could see shapes but did not know if they were the opposition. By luck the place where I actually dropped was the very track that led to our Battalion RV [rendezvous] so I had no trouble finding it. Other chaps were dropped miles away, in areas inundated by Germans. Some landed in the flooded marshes and drowned!

Lieutenant Richard Todd (Dublin),
British 6th Airborne Division

Everything on board Landing Craft Tank [LCT] went according to plan; aerial photographs helping to identify beach landmarks. When approximately one mile offshore, the Officer Commanding [OC] and I spotted what we thought to be landmarks for Number One [No. 1] troop lane. Observation became more difficult as we approached the beach owing to the smoke caused by the bombardment. When we were about 500 yards offshore the smoke cleared and I observed that our craft was approximately opposite the point where I wanted to touch down, so I said this to the Landing Craft Commander and mounted my Assault Vehicle Royal Engineers [AVRE]. As the craft came on to the beach it veered to the starboard and touched down approximately 200 yards to the right of where I had hoped it would. The Troop [six tanks] then disembarked in order. This disembarkation took place in between three and four feet of water. The first tank proceeded up the beach and started flailing just above water level. I called him up and he said he suspected mines. Shortly after this there was an explosion and he stopped.

Captain Richard Cunningham (Waterford),
79th Assault Squadron Royal Engineers

I landed on D-Day in water waist deep and waded ashore in the midst of the most incredible sight in history. The fleet of ships was terrific and my first sight of France was a church steeple with a hole clean through the side of it – a German plane appeared, and as if by magic six of ours were on his tail and down he came.

Reverend Cyril Patrick Crean (Dublin),
Chaplain 29th Armoured Brigade

The Irish were not worried about the danger; they always went for the most dangerous jobs: tanks, tail-gunners and paratroopers. The paras were full of Irish.

Joe Walsh (Athy),
715 Motor Transport Light Repair Unit

We were well trained for it; we were trained all the time. It was just like an exercise in its own way; only the ones who went down didn't get up again.

George Thompson (Belfast),
Royal Navy, attached to Commandos

The whole thing was to move fast, not to be an object for the snipers. They used to say, if you want to see your grandchildren then get off the landing craft faster than Jessie Owens [Olympic sprinter]. Seemingly I was fast.

Private Pat Gillen (Galway and Cork),
British 6th Commando Brigade

INTRODUCTION

The sound that delights the treasure hunter – the sudden bleeping of the metal detector, an audible indicator of having located a 'hard' object underground – was heard by a hopeful relic hunter seeking 'bounty' in a quarry in Haut-Mesnil, Normandy, in the early summer of 2005. Stirred into expectancy, the excitement that his quest might bear fruit was transformed and dissolved into something else completely as digging into the French soil he revealed the complete remains of a Canadian soldier. Three years later, in May 2008, after much work by the Department of Veteran Affairs, the body was identified as Ralph Tupper Ferns, who was born in Cahir, County Tipperary, on 18 June 1919.

Having grown up in Toronto, Ferns enlisted as a private in the Royal Regiment of Canada in 1941. In August 1944, he was among those having moved inland from the beaches, battling through the *bocage* countryside, the mixed woodland and pasture characteristic of parts of France, and then into the 'Falaise Pocket', where the German Army was being encircled by the Allies. He was reported missing in action on 14 August 1944 and his body never recovered, that was until sixty-one years later. It transpired that Ferns had perished during a 'blue-on-blue' friendly fire incident when RAF bombers mistakenly targeted the regiment's positions during the Allied advance. Ralph Tupper Ferns was buried with full military honours at Bretteville-Sur-Laize Canadian War Cemetery on 14 November 2008.

Thousands of Irish soldiers, both Irish-born and members of the Irish diaspora, were among the British, US and Canadian units landing in France on D-Day and beyond to Berlin, until VE Day. They played a small but significant role in driving the German Army, first from France and then back across Europe to the German capital itself. The unearthing of the remains of Ralph Tupper Ferns, like the uncovering of other such individual Irish involvements, has taken decades to emerge. Their sacrifice, contribution and effort have had to be exhumed, as it were, from the corners of Irish history. Theirs was often a narrative not related, an involvement not cherished, a recognition neither commemorated nor celebrated. Yet their sacrifice, suffering and sorrow, the fear they felt and their exposure to danger and uncertainty, was all very real.

The role of the historian is to interpret the past and be as honest, objective and truthful as possible about it. To do so you must first empty your mind of assumptions and then brutally ask yourself: is your interpretation strictly valid or is it simply how you would like it to be? To counter the latter, it is useful to first think of the strongest possible case against your interpretation and then see how your argument stands up. And if it does, then go ahead.

The Second World War continues to cast its shadow over Europe and the world. Alert since boyhood to the scope of the Irish on D-Day 6 June 1944, but knowing anecdotally that involvement to be cumulatively greater than generally acknowledged, the presentation of such participation is long overdue. Irishmen were among the British and American airborne paratroopers and glider-borne infantry landings prior to H-Hour on D-Day; they were on the beaches from dawn among the first and subsequent day-long troop invasion waves; they were in the skies above in bombers and fighter aircraft; and standing off at sea on naval ships all along the Normandy coastline. They were also prominent among the planners and commanders of the greatest military operation in history, a combined operation of greater magnitude than had ever been attempted in the history of warfare.

The scale of the amphibious invasion was unprecedented. It was a task of enormous complexity and great difficulty, an immense undertaking, both stark in its magnitude and in the realisation that if they failed, faltered or otherwise came up short in Normandy – and war is unpredictable – then the war itself might drag on for years. The story of D-Day is enormous, and the Irish have a rightful place among its many chapters. For the first time, this book facilitates the telling of this important Irish involvement and places Irish participation on the front page, by populating the undertaking through an Irish 'lens'. It builds on the prior work of Richard Doherty, Neil

Richardson, Steve O'Connor, David Truesdale, James Durney and others, especially Yvonne McEwen, Professor Geoff Roberts, Tina Neylan, Kevin Myers, Damien Shields and more, who have lately gone a good way to revealing the involvement of Irish men and women in the Second World War.

It is only a matter of time, circumstance and chance – an accident of birth, the hand of fate – that might otherwise have seen any of us placed among those on board the landing craft heading for 'Utah', 'Omaha', 'Gold', 'Juno' or 'Sword' beaches, or by equal happenstance to be in the pillboxes and other fortified concrete emplacements with weapons ready, awaiting their arrival. This is the fascination of history and it takes only a little leap of imagination to live it. Its happenings must be respected and its participants interrogated, their motives analysed and their actions assessed, and lessons learned. But first we must become aware and understand such events so that we can view the 'Irish' involvement with a dispassionate, informed and proper perspective which rightly and more fully does honour to that participation and sacrifice.

Operation Overlord, the codename for the Allied invasion of Normandy, is a day that would forever be known as D-Day. The story of D-Day is also the story of 'D-Day minus' and 'D-Day plus', and although there is no one single specific 'Irish narrative' throughout, there are sufficiently strong individual Irish involvements to justify a claim of substantive Irish participation. While in no way purporting to cast a comprehensive insight into the topic, I hope the book provides a context and clarity in the presentation of 'the D-Day Irish' that further generations can claim ownership of, and a justified, meaningful pride. By the book's end, I hope to have emptied the reader's mind of the assumption that there was no noteworthy Irish involvement in D-Day, and instead to have planted the seed that the ever-emerging evidence suggests the contrary. And I would pose the question: given the history of the Irish soldier abroad over the centuries, being as honest, objective and truthful a possible, ought we really be surprised?

Today, with the broken-down remnants of what Hitler proudly called his Atlantic Wall, the coastline of northern France still displays the disfigurement of the Normandy invasion of seventy-five years earlier. The once formidable reinforced pillboxes, gun emplacements, coastal defence batteries, mortar, machine-gun and observation bunkers are now just a ruined reminder to future generations of the bloody and terrifying battle that occurred there in 1944. The guns which once wreaked such havoc and caused so much death are now silent, and the ranks of dead soldiers, tens of thousand in number, both invader and defender, lie in graveyards close to the once blood-soaked sands where they fell.

Although there were many Allied casualties, most of those who fought there survived, continuing to participate throughout the Normandy campaign. Once the breakout from the *bocage* terrain was eventually achieved, they advanced rapidly through the rest of France into Germany. Seventy-five years later, the number of D-Day participants still alive has dwindled dramatically. Many veterans have passed from living memory, and with them their personal first-hand reminiscences have gone forever. Some were recorded by audio, visual or written means; many – most – were not.

There is an 'Irish' dimension to D-Day, but difficulties were encountered researching it. Like many soldiers who survived the Second World War, Irish veterans in particular rarely spoke about it. Many Irish served under assumed names in non-Irish regiments, among them many of the 5,000 (4,983) Irish Defence Force 'deserters', who left a neutral Ireland and joined the British Army to fight Hitler's tyrannical regime. In all it is believed that some 120,000 Irish fought with the British throughout the Second World War. There are soldiers with Irish names who died during the war, but were their families in England, America or Canada only recently there or resident for a couple of hundred years? Unlike during the First World War, the local papers in Ireland did not report on Irish casualties so it was difficult to know who the 'Irish' dead were and precisely where they were from. Many D-Day participants were not born in 1911, and so we are unable to verify who or where many were from by referring to census records. Finally, there is a lack of military service records available for that time.

But despite these challenges, the 'D-Day Irish' are no longer to be ignored or forgotten, nor is the role they played to remain undocumented or unwritten. Irish men and women of all ranks and none were involved in D-Day, and in each of the phases, facets and events of this epic story there was an Irish participation.

I
FESTUNG EUROPA (FORTRESS EUROPE)

While offence is the most decisive type of military operation, defence is stronger and the Germans had prepared well. The Allied invasion of the northern shoreline of France was inevitable, imminent even, just not today. After months of overseeing the preparation of defences to meet head-on the impending Allied attack, German General Erwin Rommel ('the Desert Fox') of Army Group B decided to leave his headquarters in the castle of the Duc Francois de Rochefoucauld at La Roche-Guyon, roughly mid-way between Paris and Normandy.

It was early morning on 4 June 1944, and he hoped to make the eight-hour journey to his home in Herrlingen, Ulm, Germany, to celebrate his wife, Lucie-Maria's, birthday with her on 6 June. A spell of unseasonal and continuing bad weather, the worst seen in June along the northern French coastline in over twenty years, had convinced Rommel that the Allied invasion was unlikely to occur over the coming days. And so, on that damp, gloomy Sunday morning after months of devising and driving defence improvements, he set out for his home via the headquarters of his superior, Field Marshal Gerd von Rundstedt, Oberbefehlshaber (OB, Commander-in-Chief) West, at Saint-Germain-en-Laye, outside Paris. Rommel knew that the Allied attack would be decisive, a turning point in the war, but what he did not realise was that the vast military machinery and apparatus of the greatest airborne and amphibious force ever assembled was in fact moving into position and about to unleash its massive might.

All too aware of the Allies intent and of what was coming, yet not knowing the details of their plans and design, proved a huge strain and an enormous, almost intolerable, burden on the German command. All their questions were about to be answered, and Rommel would be hundreds of miles away. Unexpectedly, but all too close at hand, was the moment he and his troops had been waiting months, even years for behind the vast array of concrete coastal fortifications, artillery batteries, gun emplacements, minefields, barbed wire entanglements and improvised shoreline obstacles. More than half a million men were under his command, manning coastline defences stretching 800 miles from Holland's dykes to Brittany's peninsula; even further north and south beyond that, from Norway to Spain respectively. The Fifteenth Army, his main defensive effort, was at the narrowest point of the Channel between France and England, the Pas-de-Calais. His Seventh Army, a less formidable one, was in Normandy. Whether the forthcoming battle was to be fought forward front, on the beaches, or back behind, inland of them, was hotly debated, with sharply divided views on the matter. So too were there distinct opinions as to where the invasion would occur, the Pas-de-Calais or Normandy? There was, however, a generally accepted belief that Calais was the most logical and so most likely choice. It was thought probable that the invasion would involve a support and a main attack, but where would this be?

Rommel positioned troops in improved defences, having used the time since his appointment in December 1943 well, but he desperately needed more men, more materials and more time. Most of all he needed Panzers, the feared German tanks that provided the striking power of Germany's armoured divisions throughout the war. He wanted five Panzer divisions at the coast, in position, primed and ready during the first hours of the invasion to drive the Allies back into the sea in what he foresaw as a necessarily violent and brutal defence. Not as they were held, far away and only available on Hitler's direct order. Rommel doubted not just that they would arrive in time but that they would not arrive at all. He feared they would become stalled, or more likely completely destroyed by Allied aircraft, as the Allies had almost unfettered air superiority. So on his way to Germany, he had requested and received an appointment with Hitler at Berchtesgaden to try to get these Panzers moved forward.

★★★

If the air of uncertainty, stress and tension had been temporarily lifted in the German headquarters of OB West because of the unseasonable spell of bad weather, across the Channel in the Allied headquarters in Southwick House outside Portsmouth there was rising uncertainty, strain and tension exactly because of it. Nerves were stretched further with the arrival of each new weather front coming in. Already, winds in the English Channel were exceeding twenty-five miles an hour and growing, and there seemed every possibility of an approaching Atlantic storm at sea. Mounting with the waves was doubt as to the feasibility of letting the mission armada slip anchor and head for the northern French coast.

Irish Coast guardsman and Blacksod Point lighthouse keeper Ted Sweeney and his wife Maureen had delivered a weather forecast by telephone from County Mayo's most westerly point. It was one of a number of weather stations feeding meteorological data updates into Group Captain (RAF) J.M. Stagg's Meteorological Unit at Southwick House to enable him to prepare, analyse and present advice to Allied HQ on the weather. This latest update from Blacksod Point had clarified the opinion of the heretofore divided prognosis between the US (optimistic) and British (pessimistic) meteorologist staff as to the effect of the prevailing adverse weather conditions; the successive depressions were moving eastwards. Now, twenty-four hours before the scheduled landing (H-Hour), with first-wave troops already on board ships, General Eisenhower suspended the operation and the engines of ships already out at sea were put into reverse. Meanwhile, the fleet of ships that had not yet left safe harbour were kept quayside, and the men on board waited.

With the atmosphere fraught, and becoming more so, the fate of the second front was now dependent on the weather. A second telephoned weather forecast from Blacksod suggested conditions were likely to bring a brief interlude of improved weather. General Eisenhower, so advised by Group Captain Stagg with his famous words, 'Okay, we'll go', set the invasion in motion one day after its intended launch. In the intervening years since Operation Overlord, weather satellites, improvements in computer mapping and other advances in the science of meteorology have seen the dramatic development and transformation of weather forecasting, today seen as much more accurate and reliable. Seventy-five years ago, the part played by Blacksod weather station's trustworthy reporting proved vital. A little-known but absolutely necessary 'Irish' contribution to D-Day.

Despite the weather, whenever and wherever the invasion came it was Rommel's intent to bring it to a grinding halt at the water's edge. Adolf Hitler was also convinced that the destruction of the Allied landings would be the sole decisive factor in the entire conduct of the war and would contribute significantly to its final result. Hitler had overextended himself fighting on two fronts at once, and the decision to invade Russia and his interference with his generals in the running of it saw his offensive campaign in the east grind to a halt deep inside Russian territory. As the defeats began to mount, he continued to convince himself that he could afford to trade space for time, but the shortage of men and materials were his difficulty. Hence, if he could arrest the advance of the Allies on their arrival almost as soon as their offensive in the west had begun, Hitler could buy time there; perhaps even discourage a demoralised and defeated Allied Army into reorganising and reconsidering their options, but most certainly their timetable. Perhaps even their very faith in themselves. Stop them on the shoreline; achieve an operational pause in proceedings; make a pact with Stalin and/or otherwise consolidate his still not inconsiderable military might on one front, and he could still win. As it was, most of the best of his army was in the east facing the Russians. What was in the west would have to stiffen its resistance by defending behind his impregnable Atlantic Wall, and being led by Rommel.

Strictly speaking, Field Marshal von Rundstedt (OB West) had territorial command but Rommel had sought and been granted responsibility by Hitler to inject his energies and enthusiasm into the situation. Rommel relished the challenge, and an appointment began with an inspection tour of the Atlantic Wall, only to find it far from being the impregnable 'Fortress Europe' made much of by the propagandists. A previous coastal assault on Dieppe by primarily British and Canadian forces in August 1942 had been defeated and proved costly for the Allies. A certain amount of complacence, and even willing delusion, had been taken from this by the Germans, and anyway it was believed that while Normandy was a possible invasion site, Calais had to be the most logical point for the Allies to attack. It was the shortest cross Channel route from southern England to northern France and from there through to Berlin was the most direct and so shortest supply route. So it was here that Hitler had concentrated his Atlantic Wall, strongly fortified its port, and erected significant concrete coastal defences.

Elsewhere, Rommel found many gaps, weaknesses and shortcomings along the defences of France's northern shoreline. He filled these weak points with physical barriers: pillboxes, gun emplacements (artillery set in reinforced concrete block houses), mines and yet more mines. Still, Rommel could not get enough mines and he was short also of war materials, steel and concrete and the labour force to build beach obstacles. So he improvised, creating conscript French labour battalions, felling trees from woods and designing obstacles of his own, often with mines or fused shells placed on them. These crude, simple but deadly barriers were erected in large numbers between high and low tide water marks. Effective, they were of varying types: criss-crossed lengths of steel, some from redundant railway tracks, were cut and welded together in a jagged, protruding triangular starfish shape; concrete cones called 'dragons' teeth'; another steel gate-like barrier configuration known as 'Belgian Gates'; and tree trunks, wooden beams and poles were set deep into the sand projecting seawards with mines attached. All were designed to repel the shore-bound invasion craft, to impale and rip open the hulls of landing craft or cause damage or death with exploding mines and shells. Overall, to cause disruption and confusion or to force the off-shore disembarkation of troops, thus exposing them to gunfire for longer.

Rommel also flooded large areas of open fields inland to counter would-be spots for parachutists or glider-borne troops to be dropped into. Another deterrent he used was to set poles in fields linked with barbed wire, which became known as Rommel's asparagus. It was intended that these would tear apart the flimsy gliders as they attempted to land. What preparations were possible Rommel undertook, driving his men hard and unapologetically. In so doing he intended to conduct the defence of Europe at the water's edge, firmly convinced that the first twenty-four hours of the invasion would be vital. He was going to halt the Allies as they disembarked the landing craft and bring their advance to a standstill on the blood-soaked sands; this cut short any hope of its continuance and ended any thought of invasion before it got started.

He knew that the Allies were likely to use a support attack in co-ordination with the main invasion, not necessarily simultaneously with the main assault, perhaps the former as a feint, a ruse, hoping to draw out the German reserves and instead focus their main effort in landing elsewhere. There was much German analysis of the previous Allied amphibious landings in Morocco, Sicily and Salerno and the German Army believed they had a good grasp and understanding of how the Allies intended to fight their way ashore. However thorough, methodical and credible their examinations and conclusions were, they were still left with two questions about the invasion: Where and When?

Unlike Rommel, General von Rundstedt (OB West) believed that the landings were unstoppable, but that the initial defensive efforts would be successful if they helped to delay and contain the first wave. He believed that the invasion was best dealt with after they had landed because then it would be known where to deploy their reinforcements, massed together in strength while the Allies were still disorganised, weak, confused and isolated – trying to gain footholds in separate bridgeheads. Rommel felt the reinforcements would never reach the front line, as they would be destroyed by Allied air strikes before they could be moved into place. By this stage of the war the Allies had air and sea superiority and Rommel believed this was a critical factor. The two views of defending against the invasion persisted. Convinced in his own assessment of the situation, Rommel continued to execute his preparations, making ready his course of action; not for him the paralysis of analysis. Deep down he was fearful of the unexpected, the Allies effecting something sudden and surprising. It was a battle of wits also, each side attempting to out think the other.

On Monday 5 June, 'Imminence of Invasion is not recognisable' was the tone, tenor and stated evaluation in OB West's 'Estimate of Allied Intentions', approved for despatch by Field Marshal von Rundstedt to Hitler's headquarters Oberkommando der Wehrmacht (OKW), Armed Forces High Command, later in the day. With the weather as it was, together with no apparent indicators to the contrary, they were comfortable in that assessment. In fact, many of the high-level German field commanders in OB West had been summoned to conduct a *Kriegsspiel* (a tactical exercise without troops) away from the northern French coastline to 'war game' on maps at Rennes in Brittany. Ironically, this scenario was about to unfold on the ground on 6 June at Normandy.

Having made their way to Rennes, some of the German staff car drivers congregated and tuned a radio to the frequency of a German propaganda station, 'Radio Paris', from which its German-American presenter, 'Axis Sally', would play popular wartime tunes mixed with propaganda messaging beamed towards the Allied forces, who irreverently referred to her as the 'Berlin Bitch'. Mildred Gillars was her real name and she was to serve a twelve-year sentence for treason after the war, dying in 1988 in Columbus, Ohio, at the age of eighty-seven. There was an Irish variant, William Joyce from Galway, famously known as 'Lord Haw Haw', who would introduce his pro-Nazi propaganda broadcasts with 'Germany calling, Germany calling', telling Allied and Irish listeners that 'Mangan's clock on Patrick Street, Cork is ten minutes slow' and other similar messages to unsettle and otherwise attempt to prey on the subconscious of his audience. He broadcasted several times a day throughout the entire war years, after which he was arrested and subsequently hung for treason – the last man to be so sentenced – by the British in 1946 in Wandsworth Prison in England. In 1976, his daughter, Heather Iandolo, was to succeed in having his remains brought to Bohermore Cemetery in Galway.

There was a stranger wartime tale of two Irishmen, James Brady and Frank Stinger, who joined the Royal Irish Fusiliers in 1938 and were posted together to Guernsey in the English Channel in 1940. One evening, having been denied service in a local pub, they became drunk and disorderly and received sentences of imprisonment, which they were still serving when the Germans occupied Guernsey. They were handed over to the Wehrmacht by the Guernsey Police, becoming prisoners of war. Initially taken to Camp Friesack in Brandenburg, Germany, they were subsequently put to work as farm labourers, thereafter taking up an offer of becoming members of the Waffen-SS as German soldiers. Their unit was the 502nd SS Jägar Battalion, a commando-type Special Forces unit mostly composed of foreign recruits, whose commanding officer was an Austrian, Lieutenant Colonel Otto Skorzeny, Hitler's favourite commando. He had previously been handpicked by Hitler to lead a successful glider-borne rescue of Hitler's ally Benito Mussolini from the inaccessible and highly defended Italian mountaintop hotel where he was being incarcerated, having been overthrown.

Skorzeny and his unit were to be involved in other such operations, their last major mission successfully causing mayhem and confusion during the Ardennes Offensive (Battle of the Bulge, December 1944) in Operation Greif, when German commandos' proficient in English dressed in American uniforms and infiltrated behind Allied lines in disguised tanks. They were later to cause concern when it was thought they had plans to assassinate General Eisenhower in Paris during Christmas week 1944. Such a threat was taken seriously, causing Eisenhower to be temporarily confined to his Versailles headquarters. Had the attempt been made, it may well have resulted in casualties to those around him, one notable among them being Irishwoman Kay Summersby, who served as Eisenhower's chauffeur and later as personal secretary.

Kathleen MacCarthy-Morrogh (her maiden name) spent a privileged and happy childhood in Inish Beg House, Baltimore, County Cork, with a governess, post-hunt parties, sailing, horse riding and socialising. Her father had been a lieutenant colonel in the Royal Munster Fusiliers but was thoroughly 'black Irish', as she used to say of him. A noted beauty, she moved to London in her late teens and became, among other things, a fashion model for *Worth*, the equivalent of being a supermodel today. There she married Gordon Thomas Summersby, from whom she was divorced but kept his surname. Subsequent to the outbreak of war, Kay joined the Mechanised Transport Corps and during the Blitz drove ambulances through the rubble-strewn streets in blackout conditions to horrific scenes of carnage, death and destruction, often ferrying bodies to morgues.

In May 1942, she was assigned as chauffeur to US General Eisenhower. A good driver, attractive, friendly, sociable and accomplished – in addition to possessing 'Irish' charm – a close wartime rapport was to develop between them, notwithstanding the enormous chasm in rank and an eighteen-year age difference. On one occasion, journeying by sea to Tunisia to be with him during Operation Torch, the troopship she was on, the *Strathallen*, was torpedoed and she had to abandon ship into the lifeboats. She was engaged to Major Richard 'Dick' Arnold, but he was killed while mine-clearing in Tunisia in June 1943. Kay was to become Eisenhower's secretary and, breaking protocol, military etiquette and regulations, a closeness developed, their mutual attraction evident. Wherever Eisenhower went, Kay was almost always, but discreetly, present.

That a strong relationship existed between them was never in doubt; that an actual affair ever occurred was never clear-cut. The propriety or not of this relationship was never raised in circles, but certain assumptions were made and believed. Kay accompanied General Eisenhower on 5 June 1944, as US paratroopers boarded their aircraft prior to jumping out before H-Hour on D-Day. She was also present and photographed in a US Army Group (later airbrushed out) at the formal surrender of the Germans. It was strongly speculated that Eisenhower sought counsel on the advisability of divorcing his wife Mamie to marry Kay, but was supposedly told in no uncertain terms that to do so would severely hamper any hopes of a future political career. Faced then with the choice of Kay or a career in politics, Eisenhower chose the latter. He was to be twice elected US President in the 1950s. Kay was given American citizenship and made an officer in the Women's Army Corps (WAC) of the US Army, an unusual honour for a foreign national. Kay left the army in 1947, having received a number of medals during her military career. She was to marry for a second time in 1952, to Reginald Heber Morgan, a stockbroker, but this marriage also ended in divorce six years later. It appeared that she was not to settle emotionally. Kay Summersby died of cancer at her home in Southampton, Long Island in January 1975 at the age of sixty-five. Her ashes were brought back to west Cork by her brother Seamus (himself a British Commando during the war) and scattered over the family grave.

As for her theoretical would-be assassin, Otto Skorzeny, he was to cause much intrigue. Arriving to Ireland in 1959, he purchased Martinstown House and farm in County Kildare near the Curragh. His journey there began at the war's end, ten days after Hitler committed suicide in May 1945, when Skorzeny surrendered to the Americans. He was to stand trial for war crimes in Dachau in 1947, but the case collapsed and he was acquitted. Still to face charges from other countries, he was detained but escaped. He went to Madrid and established an import/export agency, where he was suspected of being a front organisation assisting the escape of wanted Nazis from Europe to South America. He was to make many trips to Argentina, meeting President Juan Perón and becoming a bodyguard to Perón's wife Eva. Skorzeny supposedly stopped an attempt on her life and was rumoured to have had an affair with her.

Six foot four inches in height and weighing eighteen stone (114 kg), he had a distinctive scar running along his left cheek, a reminder of a duelling encounter from his student days. Arriving in Ireland for a visit in June 1957, he was to return two years later and take up residence on the Curragh. There were reported allegations that he had opened up an escape route for ex-Nazis in Spain and that his County Kildare farm was a holding facility, sheltering them, but this claim was unsubstantiated by fact. He was not to be granted permanency of residence in Ireland and returned to Madrid, dying there of cancer in 1975. As to his two Third Reich 'Irish' subordinates, having participated in clandestine raids, operations and actions, Brady, even during the Battle of Berlin in 1945, surrendered himself to the British. Brought to London, he was court-martialled and received a fifteen-year prison term, reduced when mitigation was brought to bear, he having been put into German hands by the Guernsey police. Back in Ireland in the 1950s, Stringer immigrated to Britain. Brady assumed his former real identity and both were slow, if ever, to mention their wartime experiences.

They were not the only foreigners to wear German uniforms during the war. Among the Normandy beach defenders on D-Day were Poles, Romanians, Turks and renegade Russians: Tartars and Armenians, Cossacks, Georgians and of course Germans. Together they stoically waited and watched seaward for the invasion they knew must come, and when it did they knew what they must do. From inside the pillboxes, gun emplacements and the fortified strong points behind the minefields, the barbed wire and the obstacles, they would carefully take aim and give vent to their patient determination to kill.

2
DEVISING D-DAY

Fear is cold. It causes the body temperature to drop and the heart pounds faster. Fear widens your field of vision and each intake of breath is involuntarily shallower and quicker. As the early morning light of 6 June 1944 outlined the shape of the Normandy shoreline, those in the lead landing craft felt such fear. Dawn on D-Day revealed a grey, overcast sky, a rough green coloured sea flecked with white and a vast armada. In every direction there were ships as far as the eye could see; destroyers, sloops, frigates, cargo carriers, troop carriers, warships, merchant vessels, corvettes, minesweepers and specialist craft. This was the largest amphibious assault in history. Reassuringly, overhead flew a vast array of Allied aircraft at varying heights. Spitfires, Hurricanes and P-51 Mustang fighter aircraft wove neat circular patterns in the sky while Wellington, Lancaster and 'Flying Fortress' bombers and their fighter escorts flew directly landward.

Among the tightly packed, wet, cold, nervous troops heading for shore in the landing craft were many who were nauseous with seasickness, or fear, or both. The sheer scale of the Allied assault was unprecedented. Huge naval guns pounded the coast as the lead landing craft swept towards the beaches. Overhead, the bombers targeted German defensive positions, their aerial bombardments dropping tonnes of high explosives onto preselected targets. The long-awaited attack along the coastline of northern France onto Nazi-occupied Europe had begun. Shocking in its extraordinary expanse, the scale unimaginable, the magnificence of the military might and power that was being unleashed was a sight never to be forgotten by those who witnessed it, both attackers and defenders. Wonder and awe were not the only emotions experienced; dread and foreboding were uppermost also.

For some it was an acutely held fear, with a sickening sensation of a lead lump or an empty vacant hollowness in the pit of their stomach; a chronic dizziness in their head; an inability to concentrate or hold any focused, coherent, rational thought for long in their minds. Overall it presented a potential helplessness to react and overcome the challenge of a situation that threatened to overwhelm them. It had the capacity to bring about a withdrawal into oneself, a loss of ability to control the situation and themselves within it. It was both a physical and a psychologically felt paralysis, capable of delivering a numbing, crippling, dysfunctionality if not mastered. Many in the landing craft at sea, those paratroopers and glider-borne troops in the air, as well as those within the strong points, pillboxes and gun emplacements on shore were afraid. Moving progressively closer to the proximity of danger and the increased likelihood of harm or death were mostly young men, uninitiated troops new to battle. They were suddenly confronted with the sharp realisation that war was inglorious, impersonal and arbitrary; they were very soon to learn that combat itself was random, raw and brutal, because actually fighting in a battle was all about killing or being killed. Then there were those fearing fear itself. The fear of feeling afraid is one of the biggest of all fears. There were other fears also:

> I always wished that if I got hit it would be clean and done with, that I would not be left lying screaming with a leg here or an arm there. So if I got hit cleanly it would be the first and I suppose the last that I would know about it. So that was the way I felt!
>
> *Private Tommy Meehan (Dublin),*
> *2nd Battalion, Royal Ulster Rifles.*

The reality of D-Day was the chaos of the fighting and the turmoil within the fighters, each man fearful and each man already at war with himself, as Corporal Peter Huntley, Royal Engineer Corps explained: 'I was glad I was an NCO [Non-Commissioned Officer, mostly sergeants and corporals] because when you are frightened, and we were all frightened, as an officer you cannot show it.' Stronger even than the fear of falling short of expectations, was the harbouring of a strong sense of imminent death. There were those who held a belief, a presentiment that something was going to happen, a feeling of certainty of dying. That those with such premonitions contributed to their own self-fulfilling prophecy is unknown, while others, reconciled to approaching death, were fatalistic.

D-Day was a bloody and terrifying battle; the horror of events anticipated and planned in advance. For months, even years beforehand, it was the fear of failure that occupied every waking, working moment of the D-Day invasion commanders and planners. The consequences of failure were immense and the possibility was to haunt them incessantly and insidiously. The repercussions of a fiasco, the dread of a debacle – and there were no guarantees that it would not be a washout – were huge. Doubts existed about not just the planning being flawed, but that the secret information, sensitive draft papers, maps and everything else contained therein would be either lost or stolen. To counter this, only those who were cleared with the appropriate security classification of 'BIGOT' were to catch sight of the details of Operation Overlord and other related documentation. The term 'BIGOT' was an acronym for 'British Invasion of German Occupied Territory' and denoted the highest level of security possible; above 'Secret' and even 'Top Secret'. Adherence to this highly controlled circulation of the planning documents achieved the level of military secrecy and security required, and strict compliance to the list of those 'BIGOTS' entitled to receive such material was rigidly enforced.

Working out the details of the intended invasion plan, drawing up a blueprint and developing a stratagem was an onerous process, involving much effort and difficulty. It was taxing, exacting and wearisome, yet the professional Allied military planners were well aware of the army axiom, the accepted general principle that, 'Plans are nothing but planning is everything'. As soon as you cross the start line and go on the offensive, when the first shots are fired, the plan often comes apart; war has a narrative all of its own. To further complicate matters, the 'start line' for this operation was a shoreline, a different prospect entirely and one for which the Germans had four years to prepare their defences. To rupture them, to break open the vital exits from the beach into the hinterlands, the planning had to take into consideration the assembly, equipping, training and transportation of a force capable of breaking through the German lines, as it is fighting power that achieves objectives on the battlefield. To penetrate the German defences demanded a build-up of military assets capable of exerting the application of a concentration of kinetic force so strong that it would overwhelm the defenders.

However, the plan also had to provide for being outmanoeuvred. Militarily, it would be reasonably straightforward, but the operation had to be mindful of its ability to drive off the German reserves in the inevitable counter-attack. It was about taking into account many matters all at once; time and space crucial among them, but there were so many elements vital to make the plan work: Getting the troops to shore, getting them onto the beaches, and then getting them inland in sufficient numbers with the capability to maintain their forward thrust was a start. Then the Allied forces had to join their separate footholds together into a bridgehead of sufficient width to affect an advance across northwest Europe. The planners identified, discussed and addressed the difficulties, only for more, other and further complexities to arise. The undertaking was enormous and the risks immense. There were so many uncontrollable, variable, unknown and unpredictable factors that plans relied on a mixture of 'knowns' and 'assumptions'. There was such a thing as good and bad planning; the difference between having consideration of available assets, good intelligence, enemy strengths and weaknesses, clarity of purpose, and successfully matching the tasks to be achieved with the organisation of units to do so; and of course unity of command. To add further complexity, amphibious assault is one of the most dangerous manoeuvres to effect, due to the vulnerability of the troops involved. Get the planning wrong, miss something vital or not give sufficient weight to any one of a series of different elements contained in overcoming the powerfully designed and constructed defensive positions and the subsequent wherewithal to exploit an advance inland and onwards could prove fatal to the plan and those who had to execute it.

From this the military planners identified the critical criteria, taking into consideration the necessary constraints and limitations upon which the planning priorities hinged upon or were hindered by. Understanding these and paying attention to them increased the chances of the plan succeeding. Always conscious of the fact that it was one thing to plan the fight but someone actually had to execute it, make it work, win and survive concentrated the planners' minds. In this regard attention was paid to the lunar cycle, as two requirements were considered essential; the right conditions of moonlight and tide. A late rising moon was necessary to afford cover of darkness to the first waves of the parachute drop, while offering the benefit of moonlight after they had landed. This had to coincide with a dawn low tide, so those going ashore on the beaches could best avoid the obstacles. The timing of the whole invasion depended on such factors, and these were added to the other prerequisites in order to decide the 'where' of the invasion. Away from heavily defended ports; within range of air cover; the availability of enough suitable beaches; and most importantly, at the location least expected by the enemy and thus delivering the essential element of surprise.

Translating the plan into actionable measures for the soldiers on the ground also involved the realisation that the Allies would be coming up against a new style of warfare. The Germans had reached the coast of France six weeks after they advanced into Europe, a feat unimaginable to their First World War counterparts. They had waged a new type of warfare, '*blitzkrieg*' (lightning war), a military tactic designed to create disorganisation in the enemy forces through the use of mobile forces and concentrated firepower. The Allies realised this new warfare required a new kind of 'warrior' (commandos, rangers, paratroopers) and new equipment to meet the situation, plus specialised armour to clear a way through the obstacles defending the beach for the infantry. All of this and more had to be factored into the planning. If all this wasn't enough to have to consider, or maybe because of it, an ever-present nagging doubt lingered in the minds of the planners. Was the plan good enough? Had it considered all that was foreseeable or was it going to be a costly farce? The Allies knew that the cost of getting the planning wrong could result in a catastrophe, and perhaps even lose them the war.

All in all there was a lot to be feared, both actual and imagined. The stakes were very high and all too real. The responsibilities of the role of the planners weighed heavily on their shoulders; theirs was a troubled duty, haunted by the prospect of getting it wrong. If D-Day were not to succeed, it would result in a lengthening of the war, with the stark reality of more lives lost, a continuance of Nazi tyranny in western Europe, and the continued potentially devastating effects of Hitler's V-1 flying bombs and V-2 rockets – or 'buzz-bombs' and 'doodlebugs' as the British public called them. There was also his secret weapons programme; the jet-powered fighter prototype, the Messerschmitt Me 262 and the V-3, a multi-barrelled gun capable of firing 300 lb shells across the channel at the rate of one every six seconds, the so-called 'London gun'.

The turning point of the war (after the Battle of Britain in the summer of 1940) was the Battle of Stalingrad (August 1942–February 1943) with the Soviet victory over the Germans demonstrating that the soldiers of the Wehrmacht, the 'super race', were not indestructible after all. Now the advancing Red Army was threatening the frontiers of Germany, and perhaps beyond, further westwards. Finally, there was the unthinkable prospect of the headway being made by German scientists in developing the atomic bomb. The answer to stopping this was the Allies opening the second front via the D-Day invasion of the northern coast of France, and it had to be successful.

Among those prominent in preparing the plan was Commander Rickard Charlie Donovan, Royal Navy, from Ballymore, Ferns, County Wexford. He was part of the Plans Division of those co-ordinating the services at Combined Operations, set up for the strategic and tactical planning for the reinvasion of Europe. In 1942, the chief of combined operations was Lord Louis Mountbatten (blown up by the Provisional IRA in Mullaghmore, County Sligo, in August 1979). It was a distinct and individual branch of the military that was to become a 'fourth armed service' in itself. Donovan was an exceptional staff officer in every way, and in December 1943 was promoted to Deputy Director of Combined Operations and in 1944 Senior

Deputy Director. He was one of those on the 'BIGOT' list responsible for working out the detailed planning necessary for Operation Overlord.

Rickard Donovan was a former First World War submarine commander on one of a number of small, dangerous, cramped and unhealthy submarines (L7) attacking Turkish vessels in the Dardanelles. Leaving the Royal Navy after the war, he rejoined the service during the Second World War and became one of those immersed in designing D-Day. He was retained after the war to write the history of the Combined Operations (available in the Public Records Office, Kew Gardens and London). Decidedly Irish, he was awarded the CBE by the United Kingdom on 14 June 1945 and later the Legion of Merit by the USA. He died in 1952 at the relatively young age of fifty-four, having suffered from high blood pressure, ulcers and tuberculosis (TB). He never received any recognition or honour in Ireland for his contribution, at which he was always disappointed.

Identifying problems and planning to overcome them saw those in Combined Operations drawing the strings of purism and pragmatism together. Combining new technologies and innovations to tackle the beach obstacles was just one such area of interest, one that was to bring Rickard Donovan in contact with at least two fellow Irishmen. One was Michael Morris (later Lord Killanin), a BIGOT-cleared staff officer in General Hobart's unique 79th Armoured Division, a unit that developed ingenious innovations on specially converted armoured vehicles (a tank chassis, but complete with gun turret) customised to overcome the beach obstacles. Another was General Percy Hobart, who was in fact Irish – his father was from Dublin and his mother from County Tyrone. His widowed sister, Betty, married Monty (General Bernard Law Montgomery, himself) so they were actually brothers-in-law. Michael Morris had been born in London in 1914; his father was from Spiddal, County Galway, and was killed in action on 1 September 1914 as officer commanding with the Irish Guards at Villers-Cotterêts in France. Morris was originally commissioned into a Territorial Army Unit, the Queen's Westminsters, in 1938 and he subsequently became part of the 30th Armoured Brigade as a major, Being part of the 79th Armoured Division, he was their brigade major present at Normandy on D-Day. For this wartime work he was awarded an MBE. Made Lord Killanin from the age of thirteen upon the death of his uncle, Michael Morris married (Mary)

Sheila Cathcart Dunlop from Oughterard, County Galway, who was herself awarded an MBE for her work contributing towards breaking the famous German 'Enigma' code. Lord Killanin was later to become President of the International Olympic Committee 1972–80, the director of a number of Irish companies, and together with John Ford produced a number of notable movies. He died at his home in Dublin in 1999 and was buried following a bilingual mass in the family vault in Galway.

The initiation, design and development of D-Day had a necessary geopolitical strategic context to it and it was nested, nurtured and advanced incrementally and internationally between the USA, Britain and Russia, that is between Roosevelt, Churchill and Stalin respectively, over a number of years. An early, close and long-time influential friend and advisor to Winston Churchill, particularly on his becoming Prime Minister and in his prosecution of the war against Hitler, was Irishman Brendan Bracken. Born in Templemore, County Tipperary, he was the second son of Joseph Bracken, a builder and monumental mason, member of the Irish Republican Brotherhood (IRB) and one of seven founders of the Gaelic Athletic Association (GAA, Cumann Lúthchleas Gael). Brendan Bracken chose to play down his Irish background, and over time – through the overlapping of his successful newspaper publishing career and politics – he was to become part of the British establishment and a close friend and confidant of Winston Churchill, He was Churchill's parliamentary secretary (1940) and Minister for Information (1941–5) and was subsequently elevated to the peerage as Viscount Bracken of Christchurch in 1952. Bracken played a key role behind the scenes in easing Anglo-American co-operation after the Japanese Pearl Harbor attack on 7 December 1941, when the USA had to be persuaded to concentrate initially on defeating the Nazis in Europe.

In January 1942, at the Anglo-American Conference in Washington (codenamed 'Arcadia'), Churchill and his senior military staff suggested that should the USA pursue the Pacific campaign first against Japan, it might leave Germany alone to perhaps defeat Russia and then Britain, this resulting in both Japan and Germany forming an alliance to confront America all on its own. A year later, the Casablanca Conference (January 1943) saw Churchill and Roosevelt formally agree the 'Germany First' policy for a combined Anglo-American war effort in northwest Europe.

As a result, a combined military planning cell was established in London to oversee detailed proposals for the invasion plan. Lieutenant General Frederick Morgan (British), with the title of Chief of Staff to the Supreme Allied Commander (COSSAC), was appointed with an initial staff of fifty officers from Britain, the USA and Canada to form the basis for Operation Overlord and deliberations began in March 1943. This staff was to grow to over 300 officers and 600 other ranks as they worked throughout the spring, summer and autumn of 1943.

'There it is … it won't work. I know it won't work, but you'll bloody well have to make it work' (General Alan Brooke, Chief of the Imperial General Staff to Lieutenant General Frederick Morgan (COSSAC)). Strength was to 'guarantee' success, but getting this strength to shore demanded ships and there were not enough of them available. Getting ashore and staying ashore, forcing the invasion and making it stick, became the work of COSSAC. Looking at the 'where to invade' options, selecting one, then analysing the associated problems and providing the answers kept them busy throughout 1943. This parallel military strategic planning effort developed from the Political Strategic Progress and was to further escalate after the Tehran 'Big Three' meeting of Roosevelt, Churchill and Stalin at the end of 1943.

Once convinced, the Americans were anxious to invade France, and as soon as possible. The British wanted to first 'tighten the ring around Germany' with other theatres of involvement in Italy, the Balkans and in the Mediterranean, to limit the German ability to wage war (by bombing the industrial heartland) and also to rid themselves of the Kriegsmarine's U-boat menace, before going ashore. The British effort to bring this appreciation to the Americans was aided considerably by General Alan Brooke, Chief of the Imperial General Staff from Colebrooke, County Fermanagh, the son of Sir Victor Brooke and Lady Brooke. Granted land in County Donegal during the Elizabethan era, a year after the 1641 rebellion they were rewarded with more (30,000 acres in County Fermanagh) for defending what they already had. He was among a number of British generals who had connections with Ireland and who were involved in the conduct of the war at the highest level, be it through birth, upbringing, ancestry, domicile, education or family background. None was more formidable a figure than Alan Brooke himself, whose efforts to persuade his American counterparts were important in order for them to comprehend that landing an invasion force was problematic enough, but more difficult was reinforcing, supplying and maintaining it, and that this build-up of necessary numerical strength and equipment would take time.

In his effort to make the Americans aware and understand the necessary strength needed to invade France and to maintain it there, he was amply aided by his predecessor as chief of the imperial general staff, another British general from Ireland appointed by Prime Minister Churchill as head of the British Joint Staff Mission in Washington, Field Marshal Sir John Greer Dill. Already known to and respected by General George Marshall, his once American equivalent, Dill's personality saw a fruitful working relationship develop and progress made with plans and proposals. Dill represented Prime Minister Churchill as his Minister for Defence in America and was a – perhaps 'the' – vital link in Washington in the Anglo-American Alliance from January 1942 until his untimely death in November 1944. Despite differences on both sides, Dill ensured that not only did these not become difficulties, but through his effective work that they not become injurious to his cementing the co-operation of the Alliance. When he died he was granted the privilege and unique honour of burial in Arlington Cemetery, normally only reserved for fallen US military on active service, such was the esteem and respect in which he was held by the Americans. Now buried among them is a field marshal of the British Army from Ireland, a banker's son from Lurgan, County Armagh. On the early but separate deaths of his parents, John Dill went to live with his uncle, Reverend Joseph Burton, and was educated first in Belfast's Methodist College then Cheltenham College in Gloucestershire, before entering Sandhurst.

The Anglo-American Alliance had been successfully agreed, cemented and continued, giving life to and copper fastening the D-Day planning. It can now been seen that Field Marshals Dill (Armagh) and Brooke (Fermanagh) and the Viscount Bracken (Tipperary), all from Ireland, played a background, but nonetheless vital, role in the influencing of the D-Day decision, design and delivery.

The D-Day Plan had been conceived, created and composed, and Operation Overlord had been put into place. It would not be long, however, before another pair of 'Irish eyes' saw it and the Plan was radically revised.

3
REVISING D-DAY

The British Spitfire swooped in low, only a few feet above the waves as it flew towards the Normandy coastline, armed not with cannon but with camera. This was a reconnaissance sortie, not a fighting one. Once over the shoreline the pilot banked the aircraft to starboard (right), gained height and careful not to maintain a continuous straight flight path, instead a swerving irregular one, continued on his course. The cameras capturing image after image of the landscape and what it contained: the architecture of the Atlantic Wall, the coastal defence constructions of 'Fortress Europe'. Gone before the Germans realised the Spitfire was flying overhead or could otherwise react, the pilot and his valuable cargo headed back across the Channel towards England.

The Spitfires of No. 4 Squadron and the American P-51 Mustangs of No. 2 and No. 268 Squadrons, all of No. 35 (Reconnaissance) Wing RAF, conducted over 3,000 (3,200) low-level oblique and high-level vertical 'photo recce' sorties in April and May 1944, all along the northern French coastline and beyond. They were careful to ensure that as many passed over the Pas-de-Calais as ventured over Normandy and so continued to feed German uncertainty about where exactly the imminent invasion point would be. It was important to maintain a state of confusion and keep the Germans guessing in order to keep their troop disposition dispersed, their tank divisions not concentrated and their eyes not centred on where the invasion would actually appear.

The main objective of the 'recce' sorties was, of course, to provide photographic images for the eyes of the interpreters who, with their stereoscopes, could render a 3D view from two overlapping photographs of the same image. This revealed details not otherwise perceptible and unlocked raw intelligence from 30,000 feet. The information gathered in turn underpinned the planning and provided a wealth of information about gun positions and types, construction of coastal batteries and bunkers, strong points, minefields, flooded areas, roads and hinterlands. It allowed intelligence from other sources (resistance agents, etc.) to be confirmed and supplemented, facilitating better planning options, recommendations and decision making about where to land to best penetrate the Atlantic Wall and secure a lodgement in areas suitable for expansion and reinforcement.

This was a valuable activity and helped create a substantial overview of German defences in specific detail and facilitated comparisons in relative terms, and from which recommendations resulted. Not that the photo interpreters always knew exactly what they were looking at. One alert intelligence officer noticed something unusual, and correctly sensing it might have importance brought the curious discovery to the attention of his superior officer. The image was examined, discussed and reconsidered, but it still remained a mystery. What was apparent, though, was that this mysterious object was along the coastline the Allies were planning to assault, and they needed to know what it was. It was for this scenario, among others, that the new warriors were created, Churchill initiating the 'Commandos' to be 'trained to act like packs of hounds'. Under the command of Combined Operations, paratroopers were inserted covertly from above, or commandos by amphibious means (submarines and canoes), to skilfully, stealthily and daringly execute a raid to capture whatever they were looking at. The successful raid recovered radar equipment and a detector that would provide the Germans with a warning of aerial attack. It was a significant discovery to learn that such apparatus was in their possession.

Not that this technology would make up for the lost air parity the Germans had suffered as a result of their losses at the Battle of Britain and since. The RAF, with some thirty-three Irish pilots among them, the most famous being Pat Finucane from Dublin, inflicted a significant defeat on the Luftwaffe sufficient to persuade Hitler and his generals to postpone Operation Sea Lion (*Unternehmen Seelöwe*), their planned cross-channel invasion of the United Kingdom and *Fall Grün* (Case Green), the subsequent invasion of Ireland. The invasion, if ordered, was to take place by sea, with five to six German divisions landing on a broad front between Cork and Waterford. The area between Cork and Cobh was listed as a specific 'gateway of entrance' and described as: 'Offering itself especially for the case of a peaceful or completely surprise landing, in which the considerable natural obstacle of the hinterland can be overcome before the development of any strong enemy counter-operation.'

Some of the German bombers that flew over Ireland after dropping their bombs on Britain during the early years of the war did not do so as a result of navigational error or because they were forced out over the Irish sea by the RAF. It is clear that these aircraft flew over Ireland on photoreconnaissance missions as part of the preparation for a possible invasion. At the very start of the war, on 4 September 1939, the day after hostilities began, 23-year-old pilot officer William Murphy, the son of William and Katherine Murphy of Mitchelstown, County Cork, was shot down and killed as he led a wave of RAF bombers in an attack on the German naval port of Wilhelmshaven. All four bombers were lost. The sole survivor was Irishman Laurence Slattery of Thurles, County Tipperary. Willie Murphy's death was thus both the first Irish and British military death of the Second World War and Laurence Slattery became the first and longest serving western Allied prisoner of war.

In the event, Germany invaded neither England nor Ireland, but Russia instead and now Allied troops were massing along the south coast of England to invade northern France. And so it was, in Marrakesh, Morocco, on the last day of December 1943, a month after the Tehran meeting of the 'Big Three', Roosevelt, Churchill and Stalin, with General Dwight D. Eisenhower, subsequently appointed Supreme Commander Allied Expeditionary Force, and General Bernard Law Montgomery, appointed 21st Army Group (the land component commander for the invasion of northwestern Europe). Monty was one of the best known British generals of the Second World War, distinctive for his appearance and his delivery of victory in North Africa over Rommel at the Battle of El Alamein (October–November 1942). From a family with deep roots in Moville, County Donegal, he was a professional and very serious-minded soldier who had seen service in the First World War, where he was decorated (DSO), shot and left for dead. He returned determined that the army could do better, only to be posted to 'Rebel Cork' during the Irish War of Independence (1919–21) as brigade major of the 17th Infantry Brigade stationed in Victoria Barracks (now Collins Barracks), whose conduct he considered worse now than in the Great War.

He considered the vicious underground counter insurgency of IRA ambush, Black and Tan reprisals and Auxiliary assassinations, 'lowered their standards of decency and chivalry' and was happy when the truce came. At the outbreak of the Second World War he commanded a Division in France in 1940 prior to Dunkirk (Operation Dynamo), was among the last of the British Expeditionary Force (BEF), over 225,000 men, to be brought back across the English Channel – the last to be successfully evacuated on 4 June 1940 – leaving the Axis Powers to control the European continent and poised to invade England and Ireland. Major events since had propelled Monty to the fore in the war and so it was that Churchill handed him a copy of the COSSAC Plan for Operation Overlord to review.

'Impracticable', was his immediate verdict. The Allied assault needed to be strengthened and widened. His essential revisions included more troops, more space, the US and British troops to be kept separate, that there must be a port for each and the air battle to be won before the operation was launched. The 'Plan' needed to be reworked to allow for more troops on the initial landings and the invasion front be widened, from three to five beaches, and an additional air division was required.

The COSSAC Plan and its planners were to be absorbed in the SHAEF Plan, that of the newly established Supreme Headquarters Allied Expeditionary Force under General Eisenhower. At the end of January 1944, having analysed and re-examined the COSSAC Plan in more detail, it was decided to put the invasion back one month to June 1944. This was not necessarily disadvantageous as it allowed for more of the vitally needed landing craft to be manufactured and crews trained. The COSSAC Plan had wisely taken into account what was available; the SHAEF Plan planned for what was needed, and Eisenhower had the authority to get it; the increased strength, ships and schedule (more time). Montgomery had stressed that the military strategic objective of Overlord was, after all, the main mission, that of attacking and neutralising the German military–industrial complex in the Rhine–Ruhr heartland. The question remained: by removing the 'source of danger', the means by which Germany waged war, would Hitler and the

Germans be defeated? Operation Overlord would not end with a successful invasion onto northwestern Europe, but merely begin. So begin you must, as you mean to continue, and to continue the plan must include more men, more materials and greater width (attack the beaches on a broader front).

Armies work backwards. The wished-for outcome of operations, the desired 'end state', must be kept in mind from the very beginning; it is a necessity to decide the development of the operation before ever initiating action. In other words, you must know strategically what you wish to achieve – how tactically it is to come about – before you ever cross the 'start line'. It is essential to relate what is strategically desirable to what is tactically possible with the forces at your disposal. Montgomery, reviewing the 'COSSAC Plan' in light of his experiences in the stern school of active fighting, made his revisions on the basis that the first need to be decided was how the operations on land were to be developed and then to work backwards from that to ensure that the Allies landed on the beaches in the way best suited to the needs of the achievement of the overall strategic objective.

There were those generals, British RAF Bomber Command's Commander-in-Chief Air Marshal Sir Arthur Harris and USAAF General Carl Spaatz among them, who believed firmly in the cause of independent air power and were also strong in the belief that the strategic objective could be achieved from the air alone and that Operation Overlord was therefore an unnecessary and likely costly risk. Instead, they wished to persist and indeed intensify the aerial bombing of Germany. Operation Pointblank, a specifically designed bombing campaign in support of and in advance of D-Day, diverted their attention and resources to hitting transport networks, railway junctions, stations and bridges over the Seine River to impede the reinforcement capability of the Germans to counter the Allied D-Day invaders.

The targets also included German aircraft manufacturing factories, in order to maintain the air superiority they enjoyed and remove any further German threat from the air on D-Day and thereafter. Harris and Spaatz remained unconvinced that the full weight of Allied air power should be made available to provide whatever support was required to the invasion efforts by their commanders, and General Eisenhower had to insist that

Churchill direct that such be the case. Interestingly, when giving fighter support to Allied bombers during Pointblank, the US P-51 Mustang fighter, rejuvenated with the refitting of a Rolls Royce Merlin Engine (it was previously powered by the Allison engine), shot down so many of the Luftwaffe's fighter interceptor aircraft – held back from the front but now having to deploy to defend targets specially selected to draw them out – that the Luftwaffe's fighter and bomber air capability for D-Day, and particularly more so its pilots, was seriously decimated. Come 6 June 1944, very few German aircraft (318) and pilots were left and the air superiority identified by Montgomery as necessary for D-Day was achieved, albeit indirectly.

Prior to Operation Pointblank, RAF heavy bombers, sometimes up to a thousand British aircraft at a time, bombed the industrial complexes in Germany's cities. The aim of this continued concentration of saturation 'area bombing' was to drive Germany to a state of devastation, to become dispirited and depleted to such an extent that surrender would be inevitable. Take out their industrial capacity to make war and they would have to make peace. At the same time, only at a much safer distance on the other side of the Atlantic, the American military–industrial machine was in full swing, having been cranked up to a great extent by Irish-American Henry Ford, whose father was from County Cork. Famed for introducing the use of moving assembly belts into his Model T car-manufacturing plants, this enabled an enormous increase in production to be realised. With this vertical integration, he developed mass assembly and revolutionised the manufacturing industry in America. If ever vast quantities of machines were needed in a hurry it was now. The Japanese attack on Pearl Harbor motivated Ford to begin a tremendous all-out manufacturing effort. In May 1942 in his giant Willow Run plant, Ford began to build and produce B-24 Liberator bombers on an assembly line a mile long at a rate of one plane per hour; with several hundred a month being produced. By the war's end, nearly 90,000 (86,865) complete airplanes, plus 57,851 engines and 4,291 gliders, as well as engine superchargers and generators were produced, along with tanks, armoured cars, jeeps ('Willys') and trucks, among other war materials. In all the Allies were supplied with more than one million fighting vehicles from Ford Operations in the US, Canada, UK, India, South Africa and New

Zealand. Engines for the British Mosquito and Lancaster Bombers were manufactured in Ford Plants in the United Kingdom.

Another Irish-American who contributed significantly to the war effort, through his crucial supply of the 'Higgins boat' landing craft, was New Orleans based Andrew Jackson Higgins. 'Surprise' would be provided by carefully chosen and orchestrated invasion location; 'supplies' by the huge military–industrial complex; and the third necessary element for success, 'speed', was provided by Higgins's 'Landing Craft, Vehicle and Personnel' (LCVP). 'He is the man who won the war for us,' Eisenhower said in 1964. 'If Higgins had not designed and built the LCVP, we never could have landed over an open beach. The whole strategy of the war would have been different.' It had not always been possible to put men and materials onto beaches at speed, hence the Higgins boat design and development made it feasible to do so instead of having to land only at ports and harbours. Each boat could hold up to thirty-six infantry personnel or a number of tanks; the bow ramp development allowed them to disembark forward at speed. Over 23,000 boats were produced during the Second World War.

Of Irish ancestry, Higgins was characterised as the stereotypical straight-talking whiskey drinking 'Irish' man. Surprise, supplies and speed were regarded as essential elements to achieve success in the D-Day Plan, so that the Allied Troops going ashore could outmanoeuvre and overwhelm their German opponents. That they were able to land an overwhelming number of troops, tanks and equipment in the first few days especially, was due in no small measure to the ingenuity of the life-long boat builder and designer Andrew Jackson Higgins. His LCVP transformed the options open to military commanders in the then 'modern war', allowing for amphibious landings of soldiers and equipment along enemy shorelines with both more pace and precision.

Nonetheless, once a foothold was established, in order to bring the necessary supply line into play in time, access to a port or ports would be necessary. Only there were none in Normandy. Cherbourg had been identified and targeted but realistically – militarily – it would take time to seize. Normandy as a landing site for the invasion had the disadvantage of not having port facilities available, and the planners toiled over this dilemma until they imaginatively – and initially it seemed far-fetched – suggested bringing the harbour with them. Making that idea a reality became the work of John Desmond Bernal from Nenagh, County Tipperary, a scientist and Professor of Physics at Birkbeck College, London. At the outbreak of the war, Bernal joined the Ministry of Home Security and began working on proposals for 'artificial harbours'. He was convinced of the necessity for such 'floating harbours' and persuaded Churchill of the need for them and that he could contribute to making them a reality. He suggested these could be prefabricated in sections and towed (slowly) across the Channel, then carefully positioned and sunk so that the upper sections of their reinforced concrete caissons could support, above water level, piers along which 'roadways' leading to the beaches could facilitate the rapid offloading of supplies. Similarly constructed floating breakwaters and scuttled merchant navy ships provided protection from wind, waves and bad weather. Codenamed 'Mulberry', two floating harbours were constructed requiring huge amounts of resources (including concrete from Drogheda, County Louth), a large workforce and effort. 'Mulberry A' was for use by the Americans on Omaha Beach at Saint-Laurent-sur-Mer and 'Mulberry B' was for use by the British and Canadians on Gold Beach at Arromanches-les-Bains. The Merchant Navy ships scuttled to act as breakwaters were codenamed 'Gooseberries'.

Shore to ship, then ship to shore, Operation Neptune was the naval element of Operation Overlord and it was at the High Water Mark of Ordinary Spring Tides (HWMOST) that was regarded as the established point at which the naval responsibility for the assault ceased and that of the army commenced. Warships and transport ships (including landing craft), mostly in the first wave, would be joined by supply ships and more transport ships. The warships provided naval gunfire support on the invasion and later to disrupt German counter-attacks on the beachhead. The bombardment of the beaches included counter-battery fire against German shore artillery. John Joseph Taft from Booterstown, Dublin, Royal Navy, was to be lost off the Normandy beachhead in the summer of 1944. His brother Anthony (18) was one of the very first Irish victims of the war on board the aircraft carrier HMS *Courageous*, on which were some three dozen or so Irish crew. The *Courageous* was torpedoed and sunk by German submarine U-29 on 17 September 1939 off the coast of Ireland, going down with more than 500 (519) of the crew.

The vast armada of Operation Neptune, the amphibious invasion fleet of over 6,000 (6,330) ships, had to be protected from German submarine U-boats and surface E-boats. Operation Cork, a plan to prevent U-boat packs setting sail from Brest and their bases in the Bay of Biscay and reaching the D-Day landing and support convoys was launched, whereby a 20,000 square mile area of sea from the south coast of Ireland to the mouth of the River Loire was subdivided into twelve overlapping areas, each one patrolled every thirty minutes by depth-charge dropping anti-submarine planes from Coastal Command. This would force the U-boats, known to have concentrated in their bases in anticipation of an invasion, to run submerged, deplete their batteries and reduce their top speed. In the event, fifteen U-boats set sail from Brest on the afternoon of D-Day followed by others from the Bay of Biscay. Twenty-two sightings were made by Coastal Command and over the next six days, six U-boats were sunk and six badly damaged. Their commander withdrew the remainder and no loss due to U-boats was recorded by the D-Day fleet for the entire month of June. Other forms of protection of the D-Day preparations were made to ensure that Operation Overlord remained a secret. Civilian travel between Britain and the Republic of Ireland (Éire) was stopped and a belt of coastline to a depth of ten miles (16 km) from Land's End to the Wash was sealed off to the public.

War is organised confusion, and Operation Overlord was highly dangerous and its outcome far from certain. Despite the views of the Allied 'Bomber Barons', Harris and Spaatz, wars can only be won on the ground, and one of the ways to cope with some of the confusion that war brings is to sow seeds of confusion yourself. Actuality and deception are powerful agents, especially combined with surprise, delivered with purpose, pace and precision. To achieve surprise and confusion, deception had to be deployed. The Allies mounted a programme of deception to convince the Germans what their methodical minds and logical thinking would rationally make them believe – that the invasion would be landing at Pas-de-Calais. Operation Fortune created a dummy army on the south east coast of England complete with dummy tanks, planes and ships. They created 'an army that never was' led (thus adding to the delusion) by a very real, well-known leader: Lieutenant General George S. Patton.

The First United States Army Group (FUSAG), with eleven divisions (150,000 men) were the main characters in this 'pantomime of pretence'. A false force, facilitated by a fake network of radio traffic and information supplied by agents who had been 'turned' and were now double agents, in fact working for the British as part of the Double Cross System (XX System) fed fictional intelligence through a completely imaginary network of agents. One agent in particular, codename 'Garbo', created a network of twenty-seven fictional agents, all providing information to German intelligence that the Allied invasion force would land much further up the coast than the Normandy beachhead. The aim was to keep the Germans convinced enough to weight their main defence effort opposite Pas-de-Calais, both for the D-Day landings itself and thereafter. Indeed, Allied planners believed that this fiction could be maintained even after the landings had taken place and that the Germans would believe that the Normandy landings were a feint, a diversion and Pas-de-Calais would witness the Allies' mass effort, and so the German Army would keep the bulk of their forces and tanks fixed there and away from Normandy, and not be involved in the counter-attacks on the Allied Normandy bridgehead.

To ensure they were not being triple crossed, the Allies were able to confirm their misinformation campaign was working because cryptographers at Bletchley Park had broken Germany's highly complex, supposedly impregnable, Enigma code, a stunning achievement for the Allies in their intelligence war. What is little known is that the Irish had a German codebreaking cell all of their own, led by Dr Richard J. Hayes from west Limerick. Hayes, the Director of the National Library, was a totally unassuming and mild-mannered man, albeit a colossus in cryptography. Colonel Dan Bryan, the head of Ireland's intelligence service, G2, led the secret counter-intelligence war to decode wireless messages being covertly transmitted through Morse code from a house in north Dublin owned by the German Embassy. Hayes had been seconded to Colonel Bryan's counter-intelligence programme during the Second World War for his intellectual prowess. Speaking several languages, including fluent German, Hayes was also a highly skilled mathematician.

He worked for months each day after completing his own work at the National Library, cycling to McKee Barracks on Blackhorse Avenue, trying to solve the 'Goertz Cipher' – an intricate, highly convoluted cipher similar to a code that had baffled staff in Bletchley Park. Such was its importance that the British Intelligence Service MI5 had an entire section of sixteen staff working on breaking it. However, some of the greatest code breaking minds there remained stumped. It was a code used by German spy Dr Hermann Goertz, who having been parachuted into County Meath in Ireland was detained by the Irish police (Gardaí) and held in Arbour Hill Prison where he was visited weekly by Dr Hayes. During one such visit, Hayes tricked Goertz into getting an X-ray, in the course of which he took the opportunity to search through Goertz's trouser pockets and found his cipher, proceeding thereafter, following months of effort, to crack it. He and Colonel Bryan intercepted messages from the spy and sent their own messages back to hoodwink and outwit him into revealing more information. This was then passed on to Bletchley Park. This quiet campaign contributed in no small measure towards winning the longer war.

The plan revised, the programme of deception well under way, and the provision of necessary supplies had now opened the possibility of a surprise attack, and so the opportunity for success. However, opportunity is only as great as the use made of it and it must be grasped before circumstances change. So, if the moment was not to elude them, the invasion must proceed. It was time for the fighting to start.

4
AN ACTIVE UNDERGROUND

'When in doubt, proceed with full confidence' was the phrase which sprang to mind as the German checkpoint came into view. It had not been there the day before, and caught by surprise the young girl on the bicycle was unable to turn back without looking suspicious. With the radio set in the straw basket fitted to the handlebars barely covered, her uncertainty became a feeling of grave misgiving and jeopardy. Had she been betrayed or had she somehow unconsciously betrayed herself? Insecure inside, she knew she must not reveal her anxiety; what mattered now was her ability to control her fear, endure the peril that faced her and concentrate as never before on the act of seamlessly blending in with everyone around her.

For seven months, Special Operations Executive Agent Maureen Patricia ('Paddy') O'Sullivan, codenamed 'Josette', had acted as a wireless operator for the French Resistance, along with delivering and collecting messages from colleagues for 50 km around Limoges. From Charleville Road, Rathmines, Dublin, the daughter of journalist John and his wife Adelaide, her efforts helped the *réseaux* (Resistance) network, codenamed 'Fireman', with whom she had been embedded to achieve success. Was it all now to end so suddenly, even hideously? Approaching the checkpoint, Paddy confidently proceeded to engage in animated conversation with a young German soldier who was not slow to request a date. An officer appeared, and after a lengthy conversation he too requested a later rendezvous. As Paddy cycled off, both soldiers believed they had secured a date for the evening, and both were distracted enough that they forgot to look in the basket of her bicycle.

Facing constant exposure to danger or betrayal, plus possible capture and torture, the effective existence of a Special Operations Executive (SOE) operative took a brand of bravery that was a different kind of courage to that faced by the infantryman under fire. It took fibre, nerve, strength, perseverance and an untiring devotion to make a success of the work and stay alive. The intensity of insecurity borne by the individual was not a courage shared by the camaraderie and comradeship of fellow soldiers; it was endured alone, and was all the more noteworthy because of it. Paddy O'Sullivan was to be awarded both the MBE from the British and the Croix de Guerre from the French, and she was richly deserving of both. On another occasion, shortly after D-Day in June 1944, she was stopped at a checkpoint manned by the Vichy paramilitaries (pro-German French collaborators), the Milice (the opposite to the Resistance), who were then – if it can be imagined – even more vicious than the Nazis. One of them rummaged carefully through her purse, coming within millimetres of the secret codes that if found would have condemned her to death.

Taking risks while acting alone was to be the hallmark of SOE agents. Recruited from both military and civilian circles, they necessarily had to have proficiency, indeed fluency, in the language of the country in which they operated. Set up on the instructions of Prime Minister Winston Churchill in July 1940 'to set Europe ablaze', they were led by Major General Colin Gubbins (1942–6) in the organisation's headquarters in Baker Street, London. Throughout the war F-Section (France) sent nearly 500 (470) agents into the field including thirty-seven female recruits, the only British unit to put women into the front line. Patricia O'Sullivan parachuted behind enemy lines into occupied France at night by the light of the full moon. Twenty-two other parachutes opened along with her, carrying vital weapons and equipment for the Resistance group that she was sent to support.

In all there were some 266 *réseaux* groups with approximately 150,000 *résistants* motivated by a desire to act against the occupying German forces. Small groups run on the cell structure, they became involved in sabotage, intelligence gathering and facilitation of the evasion and escape of 'downed' Allied airmen. Many became linked to the Special Operations Executive, MI6 (Special Intelligence Service) and the US Office of Strategic Services (OSS). Weighed down with a large sum of French francs, 'Josette' hit the ground so hard she thought she had broken her back before passing out. When she came around she was aware of something breathing on her face, her sudden fear subsiding as she realised it was only a curious French cow. Liaising with her contact, her SOE superior, he was not pleased that he had been sent a girl. However, it soon became apparent how intelligent, purposeful and determined 'Josette' actually was; so much so that he later refused to send her back when a male agent became available.

There were other female Irish agents working for the SOE; one already in France was 'Claudine', Irishwoman Mary Herbert, who operated in the Bordeaux area from October 1942 to November 1944. Embedded in the Resistance network codenamed 'Scientist' by the SOE, she worked in close co-operation with the local Resistance leader, Claude de Baissac. She was soon undertaking the high risk delivery of messages, even radio sets, on rail journeys from Paris to Bordeaux, during which she would place them under empty seats. On one such occasion, struggling to carry a heavy suitcase, she was intercepted leaving Bordeaux station by a German officer who gallantly carried it to the nearby tram stop for her. By May 1943, Mary and Claude de Baissac had become lovers and she was carrying his baby. When the Resistance group run by de Baissac was betrayed they had to go into hiding. 'Claudine' gave birth in a nursing home by caesarean section, fearful that she might inadvertently reveal secrets under sedation. Soon after, she disappeared, leaving her baby daughter safely behind.

Two months later the Gestapo ran her to ground in Poitiers and Mary was arrested. The Gestapo questioned her, believing her to be de Baissac's sister, not his lover, but they could not find anything of value to incriminate her in Resistance activities, such as letters, documentation and even English chocolate, which Mary had successfully hidden before being taken away. Nonetheless, Mary Herbert was held, being told that she had 'an odd accent', which she passed off as being because she had previously lived in Alexandria, Egypt and she spoke numerous languages, one of which she did not mention being her knowledge of German. This she hid from her interrogators, giving her a chance later to make her story stack up with another prisoner. This fellow Resistance member was later taken to a concentration camp in Germany when her story did not match that of her husband's. In the end, Mary Herbert was released, and having recovered her baby, she went successfully to ground. So much so that even when her family's solicitor made enquiries to them about her the SOE was unaware of her location and circumstance. Mary Herbert, 'Claudine', later married Claude de Baissac.

A further Irish SOE agent was William Cunningham from Dublin, who went by the pseudonym 'Paul de Bono'. An intriguing character, Cunningham served in the '*Légion étrangère*' (French Foreign Legion) from 1933. At the end of his term of engagement with them he began describing himself as a journalist before re-engaging for a second term with the Legion, finding himself at Sidi-bel-Abbès in Algeria before the evacuation from Dunkirk in 1940. Recruited into SOE's 'F-Section' and already familiar with weapon handling, he was taught, among other techniques, that of sabotage and was parachuted back into France as part of Operation Dressmaker in 1943 to assist with the blowing up of tanning factories in the towns of Mazamet and Graulhet. The mission had to be aborted as it was based on poor targeting intelligence and they found the factories to be no longer in production, but Cunningham's French language skills and 'on-the-ground' operating ability saw him safely extricate himself and his superior through France, then via Madrid to Gibraltar, from where they were flown back to Bristol in September 1943. It appears his SOE superiors back in London were unhappy with the outcome and William Cunningham's immediate superior was dismissed from SOE duties. Due to his French language skills and the 'field craft' displayed during their escape, Cunningham was retained, although little of him is documented.

The Irish in wartime France, those civilians already living there during the German occupation (it was estimated by the Irish Department of Foreign Affairs to be between 700 and 800 people) now had to survive under the new Nazi regime. However, some chose courageously to become involved with the Resistance and in the events around them to different degrees. The Irish became engaged in a diversity of activities, for the most part intelligence gathering and aiding 'downed' Allied air crew to evade German soldiers and escape capture. They ran considerable risks in undertaking these Resistance activities and if arrested 'in action', or informed upon, there were very real, horrible and potentially fatal consequences. It was a secret life that they took upon themselves, displaying a long lonely courage. For those who were caught, torture, captivity, execution or deportation awaited; or imprisonment in camps such as Fresnes, Ravensbrück, Mauthausen and Buchenwald. All labour camps and some of them death camps.

Perhaps one of the better-known members of the French Resistance was the writer Samuel Beckett, or 'Samson' as he was codenamed. From September 1941, as part of the Parisian 'Gloria SMH' network, he would, collate, translate, synthesise, summarise and type Resistance reports for transmission to SOE in London. Once these were ready to go, he would give them to 'Jimmy the Greek' (André Hadji Lazaro), another member of the cell, who would photograph them onto microfilm for smuggling out of France. Beckett would carry the documents the 3 km to Lazaro's apartment, this courier work requiring him to transport them clandestinely, at some considerable risk. In August 1942, Beckett and his partner, Suzanne Dechevaux-Dumesnil, had to flee their apartment on Rue des Favorites when it became clear that their network had been infiltrated by the Gestapo. Wishing to warn a friend, they went to his apartment but climbing the stairs Beckett became 'obsessed by a premonition of danger which caused them both to turn away.' In fact, the Gestapo were lying in wait for his friend, Roussel. Beckett was able to destroy the incriminating Resistance reports that he had hidden among papers connected to the writing of his book *Murphy* before evacuating the residence. Evading capture and holed up in various apartments, hotels and houses around Paris they were eventually smuggled across the demarcation line into Vichy France (that area of southern France, under Marshal Pétain, the German occupiers were happy to let their French collaborators oversee) near Les Roches Rouges, where he laid low and remained undetected for the remainder of the war. He was awarded the Croix de Guerre while twelve members of his group were shot and ninety deported.

Elizabeth 'Lilly' Hannigan, who was born in Dublin, and her sister Agnes were governesses to the Le Bret family at their mansion in Poigny-la-Forêt, west of Paris. During 1944, a Canadian bomber aircraft was 'downed' in the vicinity with two of the crew being killed and buried in the local cemetery.

The surviving crew members hid and Lilly brought food to them and helped organise their escape south to Spain, as she had done on several previous occasions. She had become involved in a Resistance unit based in Saint-Germain-en-Laye, for whom she also periodically acted as a courier, cycling with secret messages (mail) the 45 km to and from Paris. One of her main contacts was Father Kenneth Monaghan at St Joseph's Church in the Avenue Hoche, whom she frequently met after Sunday mass to pass on important messages, even though St Joseph's was also used by the Germans as a place of worship.

Having served and been decorated in the First World War, Katherine Anne McCarthy from Drimoleague, County Cork, also known as Sister Marie-Laurence, was no stranger to war. In 1940, now in the Civil Hospital of Bethane, she was tending to injured British and French soldiers wounded and left behind in the fighting as the Germans advanced across France. She aided her recovering patients to secretly leave the hospital, allowing them to get to Dunkirk and be evacuated. She also handed over recovered patients into the hands of the Resistance to evade capture and seek freedom via various escape routes. Inevitably, she became involved in the wider Resistance activities of the Musée de l'Homme (Museum of Man) Resistance movement, seeking information for them. Such activity invariably came to the notice of the Gestapo and she was arrested in June 1941 and sentenced to death on the basis of an informer's testimony. This punishment was commuted to deportation to a prison camp in Germany and over the following four years she was in various camps (Anrath, Lübeck and Cottbus) until finally she was moved to Ravensbrück concentration camp. Miraculously, she survived and was evacuated by the Red Cross. In due course she retired to County Cork.

Another McCarthy, Janet (or Janie) McCarthy from Killarney, County Kerry, an English language teacher in Paris, was a determined Resistance member all throughout 1940–5 and operated without ever coming to the attention of the Gestapo. She worked successively and successfully with four different Resistance networks belonging initially to the 'Saint Jacques' escape network. She hid many of the 'downed' Allied airmen in her apartment at 66 Rue Sainte Anne, frequently accompanying them across and outside Paris, handing them over to others in the network to bring them to freedom. On one occasion, stopped at a German checkpoint with an American pilot who had no knowledge of the French language, she passed him off convincingly as a deaf-mute. She survived the war, was awarded the 'Légion d'Honneur' in 1950 and died in 1964 in Paris, where she is buried.

Another First World War veteran was Dubliner William O'Connor, a gardener at the British Military Cemetery in Douai, who in July 1940 became a member of the 'Voix du Nord' Resistance movement. His involvement included carrying 'mail', and occasionally weapons. Arrested in September 1943 he was imprisoned in several camps (Aachen, Rheinbach and Siegburg labour camps), and suffered torture and other brutalities at the hands of the Germans; however, he survived and was released in April 1945.

In contrast, Robert Vernon (Dublin), a radio operator for the 'Alliance' resistance movement in Marseille in the very south of France, was arrested and imprisoned in February 1943 when the group was broken up by the Gestapo. He was deported to Germany under threat of a death sentence. The Irish legation in France (Vichy France), in the person of Con Cremin, intervened in the case and managed to stave off the death sentence, only for Robert Vernon to become one of thirty victims of an SS Massacre at Sonnenburg concentration camp east of Berlin on 30 January 1945.

Sam Murphy, from Belfast, belonged to and operated with a group of resistance fighters known as the Maquis. Composed of men and women who escaped into the mountains to avoid conscription into Vichy France's *Service du travail obligatoire* ('Compulsory Work Service'), they became increasingly organised into active resistance groups. Working with the 'Vény' group, Murphy would sabotage German vehicles or else steal them for use by the Resistance. He escaped the notice of the Germans and once France was liberated, joined a Battalion of Free French Forces.

One further noteworthy member of the French Resistance was John Pilkington, from Dun Laoghaire in County Dublin. A 'translator' and holder of a British passport, Pilkington was held by the Germans for several months in 1940, having a number of teeth broken, but was subsequently released. On the liberation of Paris, he took part in street battles from 19–24 August 1944, and afterwards helped to mop up any residual pockets of German resistance. Pilkington was part of a spontaneously constructed 'Resistance' group that emerged after the Allied liberation of Paris called the 'Mobile

Group Armed Voluntarily', sometimes referred to as RMA (Resistance of the Month of August).

★★★

'Setting Europe ablaze' by raids and sabotage into German-occupied territory had been the remit of the Special Operations Executive established by Winston Churchill in July 1940. Before the war was over some 7,500 agents had been rigorously selected and trained to carry out clandestine activities Europe-wide in the field and a further sixty in training camps. The closer D-Day dawned, their surreptitious support of the French Resistance was to take on a renewed focus. F (France)-Section's covert involvement had now to synchronise ever more closely and cohesively with the D-Day planning. The mayhem that its agents were causing alongside the Resistance had now to be more in line with the aims of Operation Overlord. For several months before D-Day, the Allied Air Force liaised closely with SOE in a programme of highly effective sabotage, rendering unusable the many bridges over the River Seine between Paris and the northern French coast in order to disrupt German reinforcements reaching the future Allied bridgehead. Railways too were targeted; sometimes a few pounds of explosives placed correctly had a more destructive effect than aerial bombardment.

Coded instructions in French were transmitted in regular BBC broadcasts to the Resistance underground, which once decoded had particular meaning to respective Resistance groups. However, of enormous significance was one such message on the night of 1 June 1944, which went as follows: '*Les sanglots longs des violons de l'automne*' ('The long sobs of the violins of autumn'). It was the first three lines of '*Chanson d'Automne*' (Song of Autumn) by the nineteenth-century French poet Paul Verlaine. Information from Berlin suggested strongly (in fact correctly) that this represented (a warning order) announcing the Anglo-American invasion. The last half of the message would be the next three lines of the poem; '*Blessent mon cœur d'une langueur monotone*' ('Wound my heart with a monotonous languor'). When this was broadcast it would mean that the invasion would begin within forty-eight hours, the count starting at 0000 hours of the day following the transmission.

Aware of the potential significance, the chief intelligence officer of the 15th Army Headquarters, Oberstleutnant (Lieutenant Colonel) Helmuth Meyer, whose radio interception crew had monitored the broadcast, understood its importance and had made him aware of its transmission, informed OKW, von Rundstedt's headquarters (OB West) and finally Rommel's headquarters (Army Group B). OKW assumed von Rundstedt's HQ had ordered an alert, while von Rundstedt's HQ assumed Rommel's HQ had ordered an alert. So only one army, the German 15th Army on the Pas-de-Calais, was put on readiness; the 7th Army on the coast of Normandy remained unalerted.

More than alert, and already 'actioned', were the men of the British Special Air Service (SAS), or at least some of them. Co-founded by Lieutenant Colonel Robert Blair 'Paddy' Mayne and Captain David Stirling, the SAS had proved highly effective in North Africa. With their long-range desert patrolling capability, they proved to be self-reliant at operating behind enemy lines, causing mayhem and confusion, attacking supply convoys, disrupting communications and other acts of sabotage on enemy airfields and oil fields. These were the most dedicated, highly trained and lethal soldiers of the British Army and curiously they had a very high proportion of Irish among them. For every 10,000 Irish soldiers in the British Army, twenty-eight joined the SAS, as opposed to six for every 10,000 English soldiers in the army. Some 10 per cent of all SAS personnel killed in action in northwestern Europe in 1944–5 were Irish. SAS Private Michael Joseph Brophy (22), Republic of Ireland; SAS Corporal Kinnevane (26) from the Clare–Limerick area; SAS Private Thomas James Baker (20), Cookstown, County Tyrone; SAS Private Joseph Walker (21), County Down; SAS Private William (Billy) Pearson, Croix de Guerre (22), Randalstown, County Antrim; SAS Private Howard Lutton, County Armagh; Sergeant Michael Benedict Fitzpatrick, Military Medal (27), Republic of Ireland; SAS Private George Robinson, Portadown; and SAS Private Christopher Ashe (27), Republic of Ireland, were just some of the Irish SAS killed in the liberation of Europe. What puts them apart is that with two exceptions they were all captured in uniform, tortured over several days and then shot by firing squad. The exceptions were Private Ashe, who was held for two unimaginable months in Germany before being shot on 25 November 1945, and Private Hutton, who was so badly injured that he was taken directly to Paris, where after interrogation he was murdered by means of a lethal injection. Sean Williams, the son of a Catholic distilling family from Tullamore, might well have shared the same fate, but destiny chose another end for him. During SAS training in 1944 his parachute rigging became trapped in the tail of the drop plane. The plane landed with him still attached and by the time the plane finally came to a halt, Sean Williams was dead.

It was decided to deploy those sections of the SAS who were to be involved in the D-Day operation far south in France in small individual units. There they would bolster the SOE and Resistance efforts in the creation of chaos and confusion, and they continued to sow the disruption, disorder and disarray, upheaval, bedlam and uproar in which they were all very skilled.

The Plan, the troops, the equipment, the deception, the underground, even the weather, was settled and in place, and the day of days, the 'Longest Day', that of the D-Day story, could now finally begin … and the Irish contingent among them were present, prepared and poised to play their part.

5
THE SCREAMING EAGLES

Crossing high above the dull grey water of the English Channel, the soldiers sat in silence, neither comfortable nor relaxed. There was an evident excitement in the cold aircraft but it was tempered with a queasy tension; eagerness mixed with apprehension and determination mingled with doubt. There was no singing, no wisecracks and no banter. Their feelings varied in intensity, but all were chastened with reason. They were the spearhead of the invasion, the Pathfinders, the paratroopers and the glider-borne infantry. Their subdued stillness was neither sullen not sombre in character, more a surreal seriousness.

Arriving at the French coast, the aircrafts' internal red lights went on and the jump masters ordered, 'Stand up and hook up'. However, getting to their feet was not easy; each was weighed down by eighty pounds of equipment strapped to their bodies: packs, bags, rations, weapons, ammunition, grenades, first aid kits, canteens full of water, main and reserve chutes. Below was the unknown, physically and literally; it was only known to be in the hands of a prepared enemy, an enemy that the Allied troops had to defeat.

The air armada's arrival over their target was announced to the enemy by the steady deep drone of hundreds of aircraft engines increasing in volume until it became a roar. The Germans reacted and now they were responding with flak, furiously fired by Flakvierling 38s. These 20 mm four-barrelled anti-aircraft guns filled the night sky with a deadly coloured spectacle of explosions and machine-gun tracer rounds arched through the sky; blue, green, red, pink, white and yellow. Between each trace round, the five invisible non-tracer rounds found their mark, hitting the planes' fuselages and wings, causing damage to the aircraft and injury and death to its occupants. Planes began to plunge downwards, out of control and exploding on impact with the ground. Other ordnance joined in; German 88 mm shellfire began recording 'hits' resulting in aerial fireballs. Miraculously still standing upright, those uninjured by the bombardment uneasily balanced themselves by holding firmly onto the static snap line until the 'green' light went on and the jump masters ordered: 'Go!' Out they all went, thousands of US paratroopers, Irishmen among them.

The darkness of night, the vagaries of weather (poor visibility and high winds) and the intense anti-aircraft fire, searchlights and tracer rounds of German defenders, forced the young, already nervous, inexperienced and now fearful US pilots to take evasive action. Many were untried in combat, uncomfortable with night flying and unused to bad weather, and by the time the parachute drops were to be made, they had been thrown well off course. Over 13,000 paratroopers tumbled headlong into the night, descending haphazardly from nearly 1,000 (932) Dakota C-47 military transport aircraft, hitting the ground behind where the American seaborne landing on the Normandy beach codenamed 'Utah', on the east coast of the Cotentin Peninsula, would arrive in less than six hours. Scattered, confused and disorientated, with no real idea where they were, the paratroopers of two American airborne divisions, the 82nd and 101st ('Screaming Eagles') had been sent in advance to seize and secure the causeways, roads and bridges across the flooded plains behind Utah Beach, so that having fought their way off the beach through landward exits, the planned progress of the seaborne soldiers would be unhindered.

It was not an encouraging start, the weather having played a very large part in their disarray. There were many who landed in the sea, marshes or flooded plains and drowned outright, weighed down by their heavy equipment, sometimes in only a few feet of water. Less than an hour before the paratroopers arrived, the Pathfinders had gone in ahead of them, their task to mark the drop zones (DZs) for the paratroopers to follow. Only one of the eighteen Pathfinder teams landed where it was supposed to. A cloud bank over the Channel resulted in the pilots dispersing, going above or below, too high or too low, and the 'flak' (anti-aircraft fire) forced them off their flight paths as the now terrified pilots tried to avoid being shot down. The Pathfinders' own disorganised state, some landing between two to ten miles from their destinations, prevented them from marking the drop zones with radio direction finder beacons and lights in large 'T' shapes on the ground. The US forces were responsible for the two westernmost invasion beaches, 'Utah' and 'Omaha'. The two American airborne paratrooper Divisions were to protect the western flank from counter-attacking German forces, as were the British 6th Airborne Division and Canadians on the eastern flank, fifty miles away.

★★★

One of the first, some say the very first, US paratroopers on the ground on D-Day at 0015 hours (quarter past midnight) on 6 June was the 82nd's Bob Murphy, an Irish-American member of the 505th Parachute Infantry Regiment's Pathfinder platoon, the only 'stick' to land intact on D-Day, and importantly where it was planned to, a mile west of Sainte-Mère-Église. Others – most – were far from where they should have been; they had crossed the 'start line', the first shots had been fired and the plan had fallen apart. It was here, however, that the soldiers' briefings stuck, in knowing and understanding the commander's intent. It was here where the soldiers' training told, in adapting to the circumstances – less than ideal – and still going with the mission. It was here where the soldiers' motivation and morale was demonstrated, getting on with the challenge, in the moment and in the reality that presented itself, rather than cowering down with a defeatist attitude and shrinking with faintheartedness. Instead they were defiant and determined to deliberately carry the will to win and make the best of the bad situation. They intended to do what they were sent to Normandy to do.

There was little or nothing the twenty or so American parachutists could do, coming down directly onto the village square of Sainte-Mère-Église, their arrival lit by a blazing building, one unfortunate even being sucked into and engulfed by its flames. Others were mowed down, instantly killed by the frenzied machine-gun fire of the frightened German garrison. Another (Private John Steele) found his chute became entangled in the church steeple and despite being shot in the foot, dangled there motionless for two hours pretending to be dead before the Germans realised he was not and captured him. However, dawn was to see Sainte-Mère-Église liberated by the 82nd, their objective achieved; the first French village to be freed of German occupation. The Nazi swastika that had hung from the town hall for four years was removed.

Alone or scattered into mixed groups of different units, often as few as two or three, in small fields with high hedgerows the soldiers used tin clickers (snappers), an adapted child's toy, for recognition; one click to be responded to by two clicks (more correctly 'click-clack'), to seek, find and indicate a 'friend' (as distinguished by a non-response from the German 'foe'). The 82nd Airborne Division used additional passwords: 'thunder' as the challenge and 'flash' as the response. Slowly, they gathered together into bigger mixed units and gradually made for RV (rendezvous) points and objectives in order to attack their targets. When all else failed, the more experienced paratroopers followed the sound of the gunfire. They all knew they were there to establish a defensive line, the purpose of which was the disruption of German reinforcements from reaching Utah Beach. To achieve this, the 82nd had to secure the town of Sainte-Mère-Église and block bridges, crossroads and causeways in its vicinity to deny the Germans avenues of advance towards the coast. The 101st had to mirror these tasks, only with the capture of the town of Carentan and its adjacent tactically important terrain.

General James 'Jumpin' Jim' Gavin (born in New York of Irish parents) was one of those who rounded up the dispersed paratroopers in order to form a force of sufficient strength to fight. But his first priority was to establish where exactly he was and attempt to retrieve some infantry support weapons, which had landed in the marshes and were submerged below water. At thirty-seven he was the youngest major general to command a division, and was so named 'Jumpin' Jim' because he took part in the combat jumps with the paratroopers under his command. He was to complete four operational combat jumps during the Second World War, and his orientation was to be operational and 'on the ground' with his troops. Instead of the M1 carbine rifle usually carried by officers, Jumpin' Jim carried the infantryman's weapon, the M1 Garand rifle, along with his personal sidearm. He had gained some prior notoriety because he fought against segregation in the US

Army. Sometimes called 'Slim Jim', he was commanding officer of the 82nd Airborne Division. Placed in an orphanage (Convent of Mercy) in Brooklyn when he was two years old, he was adopted and from an early age became interested in matters military and the 'commanding of troops' in particular. He saw action in Sicily, Normandy (D-Day), Arnhem and the Ardennes (the Battle of the Bulge) during the Second World War, and even later in the Korean War, and he earned a list of distinguished awards. For now, so scattered were the men of his command and those of others over an area three, perhaps four, times larger than intended that ironically their dispersal gave the Germans the impression that the combined US paratrooper force of the 82nd and 101st was much larger than actually existed.

On D-Day, the 101st Parachute Division was commanded by another Irish-American, whose Irish ancestry had possible connections in north west Cork. The officer commanding the 'Screaming Eagles' was General Anthony McAuliffe of the 101st Airborne, who later in the war was to become the hero of Bastogne during the Battle of the Bulge in the Ardennes (December 1944–January 1945) and would become famous for his one-word response to the German demand for his surrender: 'Nuts'. His commanding officer, the superior commander of VII Corps, which included the 4th and 90th Divisions assigned to Utah Beach and the 82nd and 101st Airborne Divisions, was also the son of an Irish immigrant, Major General Joseph 'Lightning Joe' Lawton Collins.

The Irish-Americans were not only among the echelons of US military high command on D-Day, they were liberally represented with some strong characters among all ranks, even colourfully so. Displaying ferocious Mohawk haircuts accompanied by facial war paint, representing a primitive and savagely wild appearance popular among some of the 101st Airborne Division personnel, Jack Agnew, born in Belfast, was a member of the 1st Demolition Section of HQ Company, 506th Parachute Infantry Regiment. Colloquially called the 'Filthy Thirteen', the wartime antics of this group in service prompted the idea for the film, *The Dirty Dozen*. Unimpressed by being dumped out of a plane right over Saint-Côme-du-Mont and a whole German garrison, Jack Agnew nonetheless landed safely but his group had to adapt quickly to try to take their objective with much reduced numbers. Everyone before him was either killed or captured, not that the interior of the C-47 was necessarily safer, with anti-aircraft flak fire coming through the floor.

With dead and injured paratroopers evident on the ground, some whimpering, others weeping, and their combined wailing potentially attracting the unwanted attention of the Germans, Agnew, who did not believe in sentiment, told them in plain language to stop or he would end it for them. The matter settled, he and his now reduced demolition group went about their business of obstructing and otherwise playing havoc with the intentions of German reinforcements to reach Utah Beach. The first thing they did was to blow up the power lines between Carentan and Cherbourg, and then they found a manhole with a telephone cable inside and blew that up. Their main objective was the destruction of a particularly strong wooden bridge over the Douve River from Carentan to the Utah beachhead, accessible to and usable by German tanks. On reaching it their demolition plans were interrupted when they were bombed by their own planes, suffering six fatalities and further reducing their number; with only four men left they completed their task.

Ed Tipper's father was from Dublin, though Tipper himself was born in Detroit. When he was 3 years old he moved back to Ireland with his family, living for a number of years in Toomebridge, County Antrim. Returning to the United States, Ed subsequently joined the 101st Airborne and dropped into Normandy with the now famed 'Band of Brothers', Easy Company, 2nd Battalion 506th Parachute Infantry Regiment. With the plane's interior light turning green and the jump master ordering 'Go!' Tipper exited the aircraft. Unfortunately, the worried pilot had not reduced the speed to that normal for exiting, so his memory of the drop was one of shock, an attached bag being ripped off, and a rapid descent before falling through a tree. Amazingly landing unhurt and managing to hold on to a bazooka (a hand-held anti-tank weapon), he landed close to a friend and before long they met up with a small group of 'unknown' others. Soon they were engaged in a firefight with a larger, better armed German patrol, whose firepower was too great for them, though they managed to retreat in good order. Later Tipper fought in Carentan, where after clearing a house, a mortar shell exploded near him, destroying his right eye and breaking his legs. Two other members of Easy Company dragged Tipper to a nearby aid station and he was sent to a hospital in England. When he had recovered, Tipper was returned to the United States.

The Niland brothers, Frederick ('Fritz'), Robert ('Bob'), Preston and Edward, along with two sisters Clarissa and Margaret, were of Irish descent from Tonawanda, New York. The four brothers served in the military during the Second World War, three in the infantry and Technical Sergeant Edward Niland as a pilot in the Army Air Force. On 16 May 1944, it was reported that Technical Sergeant Niland's B-25 Mitchell bomber had been shot down and he was reported as missing in action (MIA), presumed dead. Later, having fought through the first days of the Normandy campaign, Sergeant Frederick 'Fritz' Niland, H Company, 501st Parachute Infantry Regiment, 101st Airborne Division, went to the 82nd Airborne Regiment to see his brother, Robert, only to be told he had been killed on D-Day.

Technical Sergeant 'Bob' Niland (25) was part of D Company, 505th Parachute Infantry Regiment, 82nd Airborne Division, and he was killed in action (KIA) on 6 June 1944. He had volunteered to remain behind and act as rear-guard with two other men to hold off a German advance while his Company retreated from Neuville-au-Plain. Though the other two men survived, 'Bob' Niland was killed while manning his machine gun. The following day was no less fortunate for the Niland brothers, when near Utah Beach Second Lieutenant Preston Niland (29) 22nd Infantry Regiment, 4th Infantry Division, was also KIA. The military authorities, believing all three of his brothers to be dead, returned Fritz to home service in the United States, where he served as an MP in New York until the completion of the war. It is on this true circumstance that the 1998 Steven Spielberg film, *Saving Private Ryan*, is loosely based.

Subsequently, it transpired that Edward had not been killed in action. After his aircraft was shot down, he had parachuted from the plane and wandered the jungles of Burma before being captured by the Japanese. Imprisoned in a Japanese prisoner of war camp in Burma, he was liberated on 4 May 1945. Frederick and Edward died in 1983 and 1984, respectively.

Also part of the prelude to the largest amphibious invasion in history was 502nd Parachute Infantry Regiment Airborne Trooper James Flanagan, 101st Airborne Division. Landing near Ravenoville, he was tasked with clearing and keeping clear any German resistance along the vulnerable causeways that led inland from Utah Beach. Along with other paratroopers, Trooper Flanagan successfully assaulted Marmion's Farm, a German command post, and afterwards was photographed by an International News Service photographer with the captured German swastika flag. The photograph, with James Flanagan holding the flag in the centre of the group of 101st Airborne, was wired back to the United States and became one of the most widely distributed newspaper photographs taken from the events of D-Day, June 1944.

The circumstances of the 'capture' were typical of the events experienced by many on that day. The last to jump of his 'stick', having been the first to board the aircraft, the resultant exit was a shock. In a night sky filled with multi-coloured tracer bullets, the pilot had neither slowed down to 110 miles per hour, the safe speed at which to jump, nor maintained altitude. Landing in about four feet of water about half way between Ravenoville and Utah Beach, Trooper Flanagan – lost and alone – used his 'clicker' to find his company. None came, and neither could he orient himself on the ground from his map. When gunfire drew his attention, he moved towards it in the direction of Ravenoville. On the way he joined up with other American paratroopers with the aid of his clicker, though none were known to him. Among them was Major John P. Stopka, who organised the group and they 'took on' the attack of the German command centre at the farm complex. An hour and a half of hard fighting saw it successfully taken, and not long afterwards the International News Service photographer happened by.

In the following days, James Flanagan was involved in the taking of Carentan and the clearance, defusing and removal of booby traps and mines in Cherbourg before the end of June, being picked up by landing craft (tank) and brought back to England. He was later involved in Operation Market Garden at Sainte-Oedenrode in the Netherlands in September 1944, where he was wounded and flown back to England. Flanagan recovered in time to take part in actions at Bastogne (the Battle of the Bulge in the Ardennes). Surviving the fighting he fell victim to frostbite and was further hospitalised for two weeks. Still alive at the war's end, he married and carved out a successful career in the aviation industry.

The opening hour of D-Day was packed with chaos, horror and courage. There was always the danger of a debacle – that the Allies might get more than they bargained for – and that on 6 June 1944 the Normandy invasion might turn out to be a notorious failure and not the turning point of the war that it was intended to be. All over northern France a lot was happening at once. While the 82nd and 101st US Airborne Divisions were seizing the causeways across the flooded marshes behind Utah Beach, thereby throwing a protective cordon around the American beachhead, British and Canadian airborne troops, Irishmen among them, were hurling themselves out of planes and gliders to achieve the same objectives around the British and Canadian beaches. Off the coast of Utah, Omaha, Gold, Juno and Sword beaches, a stretch of fifty miles, 150,000 infantry were waiting in their troopships to clamber down the side netting (scramble nets) into landing craft to 'hit' the beaches at H-Hour. Overhead, bombers headed landward, ready to drop heavy ordnance all along the northern French coastline, conscious to include the Pas-de-Calais, diligently knocking out German radar stations, but careful not to 'take out' all of them. Short Stirling and Lancaster bombers from RAF Squadrons 218 and 617 (of 'Dambusters' fame after the mission in 1943 to destroy the Möhne, Eder and Sorpe dams with Barnes Wallis's 'bouncing bomb') were modified with specially designed apertures in the aircraft noses to drop 'chaff', a kind of foil that showed up on radar screens as ships to trick the remaining German radar into believing that a fleet sailing at eight knots or so was approaching the French coast near Dieppe, far from Normandy. This 'fake fleet', like the phantom First US Army Group, was an extraordinarily elaborate hoax designed to ensure that German commanders kept their attention firmly fixed on the Pas-de-Calais, while simultaneously convincing them that the pre-invasion activity under way in Normandy was only a diversion.

To further fudge German thinking, dummy rubber parachutists, nicknamed 'Ruperts', were dropped from planes far away from Normandy. These life-like, half normal size, 'paratroopers', complete with helmets and boots, had an intriguing feature; on impact with the ground they were designed to set off fireworks, simulating gunfire. Six SAS troopers jumped with them, their task being to add further realism to the deception by playing gramophone recordings of orders being given, complementary with a 'para drop' RV.

The Pathfinders, paratroopers and gliders; the bombs, chaff and dummies, were all dropped from Allied aircraft, and there were so many planes in the air that in order to avoid friendly fire incidents black and white stripes were painted on the wings and fuselage of all D-Day aircraft (necessarily completed at the last possible moment to avoid the Germans copying them). Literally thousands of paintbrushes and gallons of paint had to be secured by the War Office, with everyone – crew, officers and all others – mucking in to get the job done.

Having given the 'go', the decision to send the invasion fleet, Eisenhower despatched a message to the troops:

> You are about to embark upon the Great Crusade, toward which we have striven these many months.
>
> The eyes of the world are upon you. The hopes and prayers of liberty-loving people everywhere march with you.
>
> In company with our brave Allies and brothers-in-arms on other fronts, you will bring about the destruction of the German war machine, the elimination of Nazi tyranny over the oppressed peoples of Europe and security for ourselves in a free world.
>
> Your task will not be an easy one. Your enemy is well trained, well equipped and battle-hardened. He will fight savagely.

There was a no more 'liberty-loving' people than the Irish, and when the need was there to fight for it, the Irish individually as 'brothers-in-arms' were there, all the more remarkable because they did not have to be, and their contribution exponentially more remarkable for it.

The town of Sainte-Mère-Église had been liberated, its inhabitants set free from 'Nazi tyranny' and Eisenhower's 'Great Crusade' was underway. Surprise was made to work to initiate 'flank security' on the invasion's left (western) flank, but could it also be replicated on the right (eastern) flank?

6

THE RIFLES SEIZE AND HOLD

Alive one moment, then dead the next. In a split second, a life abruptly ended. A clean death, it was nonetheless grotesque in its suddenness. Sammy Glass, a 22-year-old member of the 1st Battalion Royal Ulster Rifles ('The Rifles') from Belfast, was struck down by a German sniper's bullet, his life arbitrarily ended. Lost to the world and himself, his possibility, potential and promise was over. A life cut short, and an ambition that would likely have witnessed him play in goal for Northern Ireland unfulfilled. Tommy Meehan, from Dublin, was beside him; it could just as easily have been him. Random chance at the choice of the sniper's target ensured Tommy Meehan lived and Sammy Glass did not. Sudden death, good fortune, uncertainty and danger were evident everywhere across Normandy before H-Hour on D-Day, only more so afterwards. This was war.

The 1st Battalion Royal Ulster Rifles, part of the 6th Airborne Division, were towed over the English Channel in Horsa A.S. 51 gliders by Sterling, Halifax, Whitley and Albemarle aircraft, and their tug ropes cast off at 5,000 feet not long after reaching the French coastline. Delivering the 6th Airborne Division behind German lines, the RAF needed 733 aircraft and 355 gliders. Once released, the glider pilots (mostly of the rank of sergeant), manoeuvred by line of sight aided only by maps and stopwatches to make their silent and surprise descent to the drop zones. At a gliding speed of 127 miles per hour, each Horsa had a capacity of twenty-four troops. While the 1st Battalion Royal Ulster Rifles (1 RUR) were airborne toward their objective, the 2nd Battalion Royal Ulster Rifles were seaborne on landing ships, heading for Sword Beach as part of the British 3rd Division, the first Division to land there. Of all of the soldiers from the US, Canadian and other British regiments involved in D-Day, the Royal Ulster Rifles was the only Regiment to deploy by both air and sea. A noteworthy distinction, a unique and deserving source of regimental pride, the individual reality for the soldiers on the ground was that they still had to fight the battles that D-Day, Normandy and thereafter presented. They had still to attack their designated objectives and contest the clashes, confrontations and conditions that combat brought.

Their specific undertaking among the 6th Airborne Division was to 'seize and hold' bridges over the River Orne and the Caen Canal at Bénouville and the Ranville Heights to the east; to 'secure then demolish' four bridges over the River Dives at Bures, Robehomme, Troarn and Varaville, in order to seal the bridgehead against counter-attacks; and finally, to 'capture and destroy' the 155 mm guns of the Merville Battery at Franceville-Plage, as these powerful guns were positioned to pour enfilade fire (from the side) onto the beachhead, thus endangering invasion ships and troops. All the tasks required daring, and some were undoubtedly more daunting than others, but none of them in any way were at all easy to accomplish. Some even had 'hidden' dangers, as Private Tommy Meehan (1 RUR) described:

> I don't understand it myself. Personally, looking back at it now, there was not a shot fired at us, we got a soft landing. We were met by one of the underground people, a woman. She was to give us the information and lead us to our objective, which was the village of Sainte-Honorine. A rumour has it, true or false, that she gave us the wrong information; that she was working for the other side.
>
> And when we got the word to charge, in we went, heroes and all, not knowing anything better I suppose, raw to action, to war itself. In we went and the whole countryside seemed to move to one side, and there they were, sitting waiting for us. At least that's how it appeared to me.
>
> And that's when the firing started and we were cut to ribbons. Fifty per cent of our battalion were killed, wounded or captured in about half an hour!

The German Army took pride in its ability to counter-attack, and the rapidity and violence of such action was their trademark. The darkness of the pre-dawn night of 6 June should have provided excellent cover for them to move forward their tanks, but no order to do so was given. However, there was some local initiative displayed and German tanks were eventually deployed against the lightly armed paratroopers and glider-borne troops of the 6th Airborne Division. Not unlike what was happening on the west flank of the invasion beach landing area, with the US paratroopers of the 82nd and 101st Airborne Divisions, so too did the British 6th Airborne Division experience difficulties due to strong winds and heavy flak. Lieutenant Leonard Wrigley, 6th Airborne from Waterford, takes up the story:

> There was chaos that day. Every unit that was fighting was a conglomerate of what fell together. I was with the Airborne troops and we did not all come down in a neat pattern. Because [the paratroopers in] the other Dakota landed down somewhere else, I was in fact responsible for the men. I was, in fact, the battle commander.
>
> So I had to hold this ground, a little hamlet just outside Ranville, to stop any tanks coming through; that was all. The [German] infantry were no problem to us; we could cut them to ribbons with our machine guns. However, we only had a few anti-tank guns.
>
> At about two in the afternoon we heard the rumble of tanks so I gave a simple order. It was the first tank that was to be knocked out. Every anti-tank gun, every bazooka [PIAT] we had was to knock out that first tank.
>
> Then the second tank would come up and we knocked that out. The third tank came up and we knocked that out. And then the [German tank column] commander, who was about twelve tanks back [must have] said, thank God for us, 'to hell with this, we're getting away from here'. Which is what I wanted.

The Projector Infantry Anti Tank (PIAT) was a British-made, hand-held portable anti-tank weapon that was heavy to carry, awkward to use and cumbersome to fire (difficult to cock and it had a powerful recoil). Cumbersome though they might be, the PIAT was still very reassuring to have available. With a reliable range of over 100 metres, it ranked as 'outstandingly effective' in the hands of paratroopers and others prepared to use it properly, and when it mattered under Lieutenant Wrigley's command, it was. Having been seized, Ranville village was held. It was sometimes as a consequence of such attacks that German prisoners were taken and how they were treated by the Allies was generally determined by how they behaved themselves. 'I never saw a German Prisoner of War shot', said Lieutenant Wrigley. 'I do not believe any Allied officer would shoot a German with his hands up.'

Private Tommy Meehan was to have an entirely different experience of surrendering Germans: 'These three fellows came out of the woods with their hands up carrying a white handkerchief or towel. I recognised a grenade under the handkerchief and I shouted "Dive!" As we dived we shot the three of them and the grenade went off. He was prepared to kill us if we had let our guard down.'

Paratrooper Jack McCormack, from Newbridge, County Kildare, was dropped on D-Day with one day's supply of food and water. Thereafter, the Allied invading forces from the beaches were to link up with them and supplies made available. Instead, it was nearly a full week – six days – before Paratrooper McCormack and those with him were relieved. In the interim they had to drink water out of ditches, and for much of that time they were under constant attack from the Germans, the most nerve-racking experience was coming under mortar fire. He was to be wounded twice in the fighting, one bullet hitting his nose, flattening it and chipping off a slight piece of bone, the second wound was more serious. A German sniper concealed in a bell tower shot him in the left arm, blowing apart his bicep muscle. Taken from the field, he was transferred back to hospital in England. He was to lose some power in his arm and would have to wear a brace for the rest of his life.

Like the US paratroopers, the British paratroopers employed Pathfinders ahead of the main troop drop to guide the bulk of the airborne assault onto the selected drop zones. Among the 22nd Independent Parachute Company, the Pathfinders for the 6th Airborne Division, was Lance Corporal Edward O'Sullivan. He landed near Touffreville not long after midnight and infiltrated the town. At 4 am his body was found by two French boys, ten yards from the body of a dead German. It is believed that the two men killed each other simultaneously with their submachine guns. The grateful villagers named a square in the town after him.

★★★

Undoubtedly, one of the most daring and well executed actions by the 6th Airborne Division was the raid involving the seizure of what was subsequently renamed Pegasus Bridge. In reality, the prize was two bridges that were required to be seized intact, the Bénouville Canal de Caen Bridge (renamed Pegasus Bridge after the Paratrooper Regiment insignia) and the Ranville (river bridge). A 'coup-de-main' operation, a swift attack that relies on speed and surprise to accomplish its objectives, was the specific task of 180 men from the 2nd Oxfordshire and Buckinghamshire Light Infantry (the Ox and Bucks) and 249 Field Company Royal Engineers, all commanded by Major John Howard. Crash-landing their gliders with expert precision immediately adjacent to the bridge, they surprised a stunned guard and overwhelmed them with staggering speed and suddenness, grenades and small-arms fire, no small feat in itself. Successfully seized in ten minutes, it would be far harder to hold. Among those seizing the bridges were six men from Ireland; there was an O'Neill, O'Donnell, O'Shaughnessy, Keane, Anton and Ferguson. In fact, 10 per cent of the 'Ox and Bucks' were from Ireland.

The plan was for the 7th Parachute Regiment to land and reinforce them and together they would withstand any attempted German counter-attacks until further reinforced by Lord Lovat's 1st Special Service (Commando) Brigade due to land on Sword Beach, west of Ouistreham, six miles distant. Shortly after dawn, with the airborne forces scattered in various widely dispersed directions, far-flung and separated, the 7th Battalion nonetheless mustered 200 men within thirty minutes to support the bridge holders and together set about its defence. Meanwhile, others of the 7th Parachute Battalion arrived through the darkness, individually or in small groups, further bolstering the numbers. Major Howard and his men positioned themselves between the bridges, acting as reserve to those now situated around the position's perimeter. One of the very first to arrive was 24-year-old Dublin-born Captain Richard Todd. His father, Major Andrew Todd, played international rugby for Ireland, earning three caps, and was a doctor in the British Army. Not long after Richard Todd's arrival, in fact coinciding with it, was a push by the Germans to retake the bridges. This was one of several German attacks that had to be repelled: 'We got to Pegasus Bridge at the same moment as the German reaction opened up. There was a lot of firing and we lost sixty-five men on the bridge.' Exhausted, they were to fight for almost a full day (twenty-one hours) before being relieved at 2200 hours (10 pm), late on D-Day.

Deserving of credit for the spectacularly successful seizure of the two bridges by Major Howard and his men from the Ox and Bucks, it was perhaps the lesser known defence over that subsequent twenty-one hours by Lieutenant Colonel Geoffrey Pine-Coffin which was equally (perhaps more so) meritorious, and the men of the 7th Parachute Regiment, Irishmen among them, demonstrated stalwart soldiering skills in so doing. The quickest and surest way of seizing the bridges and other objectives was by airborne assault, and now in Allied hands they had to be kept. The only two crossing points between the coastline and Caen secured, it was vital that they were held. Further east, a mile north of Ranville, an important ridgeline whose capture had been imperative was reinforced by some seventy glider loads of paratroopers from the 5th Paratroop Brigade at 0330 hours (3.30 am) bringing with them crucial support weapons, heavy machine guns and both six- and seventeen-pounder anti-tank guns. Somewhat further east again, the River Dives valley had been flooded by the Germans to deter airborne landings. By capturing and destroying the four bridges over the river the British had turned this tactical disadvantage around to a tactical advantage, the end result contributing significantly towards hindering any possible German reinforcements from the east, particularly of armour.

This task had been given and successfully carried out by the 3rd Parachute Brigade, but they had another mission and put in charge of its execution was Lieutenant Colonel Terence Otway, 9th Parachute Battalion, who had Irish ancestors from County Laois. This was the taking and destruction of the Merville Gun Battery, perhaps the most dangerous mission of all given to the 6th Airborne Division. Formerly of the Royal Ulster Rifles, on receipt of his orders Lieutenant Colonel Otway had two months to plan, prepare and rehearse for the operation. This even involved landscaping a life-size model of the objective, simulating the shape, form, line and contours of the terrain wherein it rested. The information was obtained from aerial photographs, and the physical configuration of the terrain was reproduced by bulldozers and mechanical excavators.

His entire Battalion, of over thirty officers and 600 of all ranks, rehearsed relentlessly, day and night, with blank and real ammunition, until everyone was not only familiar with the role each had to play, but highly proficient in it. No. 2 Troop 591 (Antrim) Parachute Squadron Royal Engineers, with volunteers from 9th Battalion, were to crash land in three gliders on top of the battery. This was only one element of an elaborate plan which saw Otway divide his force into eleven separate parties, each with a definite task to fulfil. These included minefield and barbed wire breaching, assault, fire base support, reserve and vanguard. The assault was sequenced with a prior aerial bombardment by 100 Lancasters, and should the attack fail, a naval bombardment was organised to commence firing at 0530 hours. If the raid was successful, yellow flares were to be sent skywards obviating the need for the naval salvos. The prepared plan was complex and involved, elaborate and intricate, and all of the elements covered as many possible contingencies as could be considered. It was essential that the battery was destroyed by 0530 hours (5.30 am), thirty minutes prior to H-Hour. Timings dictated the attack commence at 0430 hours (4.30 am) so Otway and the 9th Parachute Battalion had one hour to successfully complete their mission.

Major General Richard 'Windy' Gale, commander of the 6th Airborne Division, described the Merville Battery's importance as an objective:

> It was so situated that it could fire on the beaches, as well as on the sea approaches to them in which 1 Corps assault divisions were to land. Our task was to seize and silence this battery before the assault craft came within its range. The sea assault was to be at dawn, and nothing could have been more awful to contemplate than the havoc this battery might wreak on the assault craft as they slowly forged their way to the shore. It was of course hoped that bombing alone could achieve this [but] the actual guns were in enormous reinforced concrete casements and nothing but a direct hit from one of the heaviest bombs would knock them out. That meant that each gun in turn would have to be hit. One raid would never achieve this; and prolonged bombing of

the battery would be the best way of indicating to the Germans the left flank of the Allied invasion. The whole of the northern coast of France was studded with such batteries. A similar treatment of the others as a bluff would use too much of our bomber effort, which was required for a multitude of other tasks. For these reasons a direct assault on the battery by airborne troops was necessary.

As Lieutenant Colonel Richard Otway saw his assault plan:

The Battery contained four guns which were thought to be 155 mm, and each gun was in an emplacement made of concrete six-foot thick, on top of which was another six-foot of earth. There were steel doors in front and rear. The garrison was believed to consist of 150–200 men, with two 20 mm dual purpose guns and up to a dozen machine guns. There was an underground control room and odd concrete pillboxes dotted about. The position was circular, about 400 yards in diameter, and surrounded by barbed wire and mines. There was a village a few hundred yards away which might have held more German troops. There were only two sides from which we could possibly attack. On the north there was a double apron barbed wire fence, outside which was a minefield about thirty yards deep. Outside this again was an anti-tank ditch fourteen feet wide and sixteen feet deep, which we assumed would be full of horrors. On the south side there was the same double apron fence and the same thirty yard minefield, but instead of the ditch there was another barbed wire fence some twelve to fifteen feet thick and five to six feet high. The whole battery was then surrounded by a minefield 100 yards deep, which was protected by a barbed wire cattle fence, probably electrified. Such was the nut to be cracked. As we were to land to the south of the Battery, I decided to attack from the south. The basis of my plan was surprise and the fact that I did not intend to allow the garrison to concentrate on any one point; they would have to look several ways at once.

The assault plan drawn up in detail, each man was made aware of the means of achieving the objective, the scheme rehearsed and the attack methodology practised repeatedly; it was time to execute. Before they departed, Brigadier James Hill, 3rd Parachute Brigade, 6th Airborne Division, addressed his charges with the following prophetic words: 'Gentlemen, do not be daunted if chaos reigns; it undoubtedly will.' It did – it was a shambles! A dreadful drop, the 9th Parachute Battalion was hopelessly scattered and their cohesion fractured. Undeterred, Lieutenant Colonel Otway, without most of the specialist equipment needed yet conscious of the mission's importance and the pressing time requirement, headed for the rendezvous point. There he found that only some 25 per cent, 150 out of 600 of his 'attack force', had successfully made it. Adapting the attack plan, he adjusted the assault to suit the new circumstances; there was no lessening of the assertiveness required or the aggression to be applied to the action.

Lieutenant Mike Dowling, B Company, 9th Parachute Battalion, with Irish connections in County Tipperary, was part of the altered assault assembly. He was in charge of one of the four much-reduced teams, in his case set to attack gun casement No. 2. The Lancaster's had dropped their bombs and departed, leaving the landscape pockmarked with many craters, debris and dead cows. The diversionary attack commenced and the attack teams, supported by their fire bases and snipers, ran along the pathway cleared through the minefield, through the gap in the barbed wire blown by the Bangalore torpedoes, and dashed forward to the guns – even running in and out of bomb craters. Fire opened up on them and not everyone kept moving forward. The Battalion second-in-command, Major Parry, went down and several of his group were hit as they charged headlong in their advance toward the gun casements. They replied with Sten guns and threw '77' phosphorous grenades. Making it to the casements, they announced their arrival by tossing grenades into their interiors and blazing away with their Sten guns. The defenders quickly ceased fire, they had been surprised and overwhelmed.

The objective had been secured, the darkness and confusion helping their cause. Now to see to the German prisoners, take care of their own wounded and of course set about disabling the guns. Explosions followed and the destruction of the battery was complete. There was an element of disappointment, too. The guns were not the mighty 155 mm weapons they were expecting, rather they were of reduced calibre. However, there was no time to muse on matters as incoming heavy and accurate mortar and shellfire meant withdrawal was paramount. Not all of the British wounded could be carried out and some were left in the care of the Germans; there was simply no choice.

Lieutenant Mike Dowling went up to Lieutenant Colonel Otway, his right hand and arm over his chest covering a wound suffered during the charge. Saluting, he said, 'Battery taken as ordered, Sir,' and then dropped down dead. Three of the guns had been destroyed by Gammon bombs, an explosive charge wrapped in fabric and sewn to an impact fuse that was especially suitable for the destruction of aircraft or vehicles, and one by firing two shells at once through the barrel of the gun. The 'success' signal was lit at 0500 hours, indicating that the naval bombardment by HMS *Arethusa* was not needed. On withdrawal, a check on personnel revealed that one officer had been killed, four wounded and sixty-five other ranks were killed, wounded or missing. About eighty men were still standing and operational. Private 'Paddy' Roche (20) suffered a shrapnel wound in the back, was evacuated and operated on, but died of shock at 6 pm on 10 June. He is buried in Ranville cemetery (Grave 1AE3). Private John 'Paddy' McSorley (27) died on 12 June while attacking German tanks with a PIAT. He is also buried in Ranville cemetery (Grave IAF20).

Coming into contact with the enemy and containing it, engaging in a firefight and winning it were not everyday occurrences, but all of the Allied forces were prepared to make the ultimate sacrifice, as Lieutenant Leonard Wrigley explains: 'There were oceans of blood for the people who were actually fighting. One illustration of this is that of the 26,000 who landed before 6 am, 12,000 were either dead or wounded by 6 pm that evening.'

The adverse effects of battle were described differently by Private Tommy Meehan (1 RUR): 'I do not know how long it took to get used to it, but you had to get used to it. It was not very pleasant to come across someone with their guts torn out; a man with his arm, leg or even head blown off for that matter. No, it was not pleasant.' Neither were the effects only physical; he also recalled: 'I saw one fellow being led away. "Bomb Happy", we called it, with his nerve gone due to the constant shelling. That was a sight to behold, and he such a tough nut himself, to see him being led away like a child crying for his mummy.' Another instance is described by Peter Huntley,

Royal Engineers: 'We had a wonderful captain, and he just lost all his nerve. And broke down and had to be sent back to England. We never saw him again.'

Affected differently, but not adversely, was Private Paddy Devlin, 1st Battalion Royal Ulster Rifles. From Moycullen, County Galway, Private Devlin was one of those who landed by glider, and when he looked up at the arriving Allied aerial armada he was so overwhelmed by the sight of hundreds of planes flying overhead that he quite forgot his orders to deploy. Among them was Rifleman James Durham (19), of Rathmines, Dublin, who landed in Normandy on D-Day at 2100 hours (9 pm) as part of the glider-borne reinforcements sent to consolidate the successes of the men who had been fighting since dawn. Landing around Longueval, he and his comrades were sent in to secure the village. Once secured, they pressed on to capture Sainte-Honorine, where much stiffer German opposition was encountered. In the subsequent firefight they were forced back to the earlier captured Longueval. Rifleman Durham was shot in the legs and feet by enemy fire and was helped there by comrades. He had very nearly been left behind, as in their hasty retreat the British could only take the 'walking wounded'. But a friend recognised him and helped him back to safety. Removed to an army hospital in England, his leg was saved from amputation by the skill of a surgeon, and after two years of recuperation in England, he surprised his sister and mother by knocking on their door at Christmas. A happy ending for one Irishman, who nearly fell victim to the battlefields of Normandy.

7
ANGRIFF! ANGRIFF! (RAID! RAID!)

Aware that the time to experience war was approaching, probably sooner rather than later, those Germans stationed in France were not unhappy to be there. The alternative was to be on the Eastern Front, fighting against the Russians. With the harsh winters, hot summers and hard combat of the Eastern Front – often both gruelling and gruesome – and with exposure to arduous and abhorrent conditions, they considered themselves fortunate to find themselves in a situation with no ongoing fighting, a mild climate, access to food and having the minimum of at least a passing relationship, and often better, with the local population. Of course, they were aware that an invasion was coming, and logically it had to be this summer (1944) and every passing day made its arrival ever more imminent. They had become used to the sound of nightly bombing along the coast, bombers flying overhead and the occasional small-scale actions of the Resistance. They were also conscious of the German propaganda 'messaging' and many believed they were not merely 'defending' France, but Germany, their homes and families and 'the Reich'. If the Allies were preparing to invade, they were ready to meet them.

The Germans stationed along the Atlantic Wall on the northern French coastline knew they would soon be called upon to repulse – to drive back by force – the Allied attack from whence it came. For their part the Germans were in static defences, in concrete constructs behind deliberately designed, purpose-built integrated structures of solid stone and steel. Since the uptake of his appointment, Rommel had succeeded in intensifying the preparations of these fortifications, the minefields and the tank traps, as effectively as anyone else, if not more so. Conscript workers, forced labour from eastern Europe – Russians, Hungarians and Polish – and of course from France itself, were worked incessantly round the clock. Large anti-tank ditches were dug, then made deeper, minefields were laid, then enlarged, bunkers were built, then further reinforced; all to channel attacking Allied troops, but their tanks more especially, to within range of carefully sited anti-tank weapons (PAK) and powerful MG 42 machine guns.

In addition to being placed in bunkers, these were sited on the ground floors of 'fortified houses', beachfront villas or a little inland, in farmhouses and other 'strong point' structures. Those buildings considered suitable for adaptation and sited tactically were identified and such properties were laid claim to – requisitioned by the German military – and emptied of the occupying French families. Once taken possession of their structures were strengthened and then bolstered and buttressed with logs, sandbagged earth and concrete. Already strongly constructed, these buildings had sturdy stone walls and were ideal for adaptation. In some instances, almost entire small coastal and inland villages were turned into fortresses. A series of outlying smaller single-man 'Tobruk' bunkers, small concrete machine-gun posts first used by the Italian Army in Libya and adapted by Rommel for use on the Atlantic Wall, were positioned in support of the larger fortified buildings and bunkers, built into existing earth mounds or dug in below ground level for easy cover and concealment.

The bunkers were usually placed in dugout holes three metres square, two metres deep and cased in concrete, often prefabricated. This hollow concrete block interior was entirely below ground, above it was a camouflaged cupola cover with a circular opening and a mounting for a smaller but still lethally effective MG 34 machine gun. An alternative two-man version was mounted with a tank turret on top, usually from an old French or Czech tank. These one- and two-man 'Tobruk' bunkers were sited at places of tactical significance, at crossroads and for local defence covering rear approaches to the larger 'strong houses' or 'fortified houses' or to protect searchlight installations and flak batteries.

Inland of the beach defences, depth was added with a further line of fall-back bunkers and fortified strong houses and 'Widerstandsnest' (resistance points). These were placed along the coastline and inland. They were a concrete-faced trench, usually thirty metres long by ten metres wide, topped with a raised concrete parapet one metre in height, dug into the ground to afford their German occupants the ability to adopt a protected standing position for firing. There were a number of trenches running rearwards in a zig-zag fashion. Two MG 42 machine-gun firing points with vertical slits at either end added to the firepower capacity that these 'resistance points' could pour onto Allied attackers, sited as they were with good fields of fire on hilltops and clifftops. The Atlantic Wall artillery gun emplacement defences were either beach batteries or large inland coastal batteries. The beach batteries fired at craft approaching in the shallows or on targets (tanks and infantry) on the beach itself from bunkers sited to deliver enfilade fire from the side. The much larger inland coastal batteries were equipped with bigger calibre guns to engage naval targets at longer ranges out to sea.

Hence, the German defences extended from the low tide mark, with anti-landing beach obstacles, mines and barbed wire in combination with a belt of shore-sited bunkers, behind which inland were lines of 'fortified houses' and further inland still a layer of fortified villages linked together with bunkers, 'resistance points' and 'Tobruk' bunkers. This belt of blockades was a serious stumbling block and an impressive impediment for the Allied troops aimed at disrupting any attempted landing on and breakout from the beaches. The lines of beach and coastal defences became known as 'Satan's Garden', and it was here that the holding back of any Allied armour would occur, not necessarily indefinitely but for long enough to allow the Panzer reserves to be brought forward and deployed. And then with their combined firepower they could push the invasion back into the sea.

'Panzerfausts' (anti-tank rockets); 'Panzerschreck' (hand-held anti-tank bazookas) and 'Goliaths' were additional close-in anti-armour assets available to the defenders. The 'Goliath' was a remotely controlled small tracked vehicle, about the size of a wheelbarrow, filled with explosives which once (wire) guided close to an Allied tank would be detonated. Deployed from hidden bunkers along the beachfront against tanks or grouped infantry, when activated its detonation blast wave would cause a high degree of devastation. Originally designed for offensive purposes, the Germans had adapted its use to aid their defensive posture along the Atlantic Wall. The entire landscape had been shaped and moulded into a massive 'killing ground' to minimise the Allied attack options, curtail tank movement and channel troops into areas prepared to maximise arcs of interlocking anti-tank and machine-gun defensive fire. Ready and rehearsed, the Germans were waiting for the Allies to arrive.

There seemed no reason why the Allies had not invaded during May, and this apprehension was heightened with each passing week. Not quite on tenterhooks, there was nonetheless an anxiety felt by many. That this state of suspension was not one of alarm was tempered by the belief that any 'invasion armada' would involve the capture and use of existing ports and harbours, and a pure beach landing was impossible. And so, mixed with the general feeling that something would happen soon, a landing on the Normandy beaches, whose defence was their mission, was considered highly unlikely by those defending them.

Almost as soon as it had become dark on the night of 5 June, the increase in the amount of Allied air activity overhead had been very noticeable to the German defenders posted to units manning the Atlantic Wall. The bombing south and east of them, which had been on the rise over the preceding weeks, was now intense and the noise of aircraft engines was constant. Not yet in receipt of reports that paratroopers were being dropped south behind them from out of the night sky – if any were received they were intermittent, confused and were not causing alarm – they were also unaware that just over the horizon, coming directly at them, was an Allied invasion armada that logically should not be there. The defenders would shortly be relieved of their anxious boredom; replaced suddenly with acute battle!

Out of the misty, murky, grey light of a cold, 'dirty' dawn, appeared indistinct, shadowy silhouettes. The outlines of tanks 'swimming' on the surface of the sea, independently powered and self-supporting, the closer they came the more apparent that it was actually true. Shock replaced surprise as the floating tanks headed for shore from an invasion armada that came from nowhere; where reason dictated it ought not to be! These were an Allied secret weapon, the Duplex Drive (DD) Sherman tanks, or amphibious 'Donald Duck' tanks as the Americans called them. They were 'invented' so that tanks could land alongside, even ahead of, infantry in places where it was neither possible, nor advisable for the beaching of larger landing ships. This was one way that the Allies could force their way inland, and hundreds of them were to see action on D-Day, though not all would make it to the beaches.

That the Allies would select Utah Beach, with its immediately adjacent flooded plains behind it, was further reason for the German defenders' disbelief, as the American 4th Infantry Division came towards them out of the dawn. The area behind Utah Beach itself, a ten-mile stretch of open, smoothly shelving sand for up to two miles inland, had been both flooded and mined. This area was a massive mined marsh, and access to the beach was restricted to five narrow causeways leading to the villages of Audouville-la-Hubert, Saint-Germain, Pierreville and Saint-Martin-de-Varreville. It was onto these five causeways that the 82nd and 101st Airborne Divisions had dropped from the night sky earlier that morning, to secure along with other objectives. Once the now-landing 4th Infantry Division had overwhelmed the beach defences, they would advance inland along these causeways. That at least was the plan, the first part of which had been achieved pre-dawn by the US paratroopers.

To help 'the Ivy Leaves' as the US 4th Infantry Division was called, were thirty-two DD tanks and armoured bulldozers. The Americans had opted not to use the full range of specialised obstacle-clearing armoured vehicles developed by the British 79th Armoured Division, which included the 'crab' tank, with a front attachment supporting a huge chained flail that literally spun around beating a path through minefields, exploding them where they were laid and thus making it safe for other tanks and infantry to follow in its path. 'Bobbin' tanks would lay out a carpet of tracking across muddy terrain, marsh or soft sand, and 'Crocodile' tanks were adapted with flamethrowers for use against the enemy bunkers. 'Fascine' tanks carried logs to fill in anti-tank ditches and bomb craters; small 'box girder' tanks with mini bridge lengths made of steel, were made to cross gaps. These were based on the British Churchill tank, as was the 'Petard' tank, whose bunker-busting spigot mortar (290 mm 'flying dustbins') would come into play to move a situation on should any particular enemy bunker prove itself obstinate. The British

'Firefly' Sherman tank mounted with the British 17-pounder anti-tank gun, a match for German 'Panther' and 'Tiger' tanks armed with their 88 mm guns, were very effective and were in demand but scarce. The numbers available were insufficient to arm more than one for every tank troop.

It was these 'machines' over which Irishmen Percy Hobart and Michael Morris (Lord Killanin) had oversight, and on D-Day itself using a BSA motorbike Michael Morris went ashore to oversee their effectiveness in actual combat conditions. There were other variants, like the Churchill Armoured Ramp Carrier, which by extending ramps at either end could transform itself into a bridge (or ramp) over which other vehicles could traverse. There was also the 'Double Orion' demolition explosive charge-carrying armoured tank, a vehicle which allowed for the carrying of 'Bangalore Torpedoes', lengths of pipe filled with explosives (extendable to the distance required by adding further lengths) for use against barbed wire and other obstacles. Montgomery had decided that in the actual moment of assault, rather unconventionally, the infantry needed the support of the tanks – not only with them, but actually ahead of them – hence the DD 'swimming tanks' were sent in first with the AVRE 'specialised' tanks ahead of them as they landed.

Operation Overlord involved the execution of five interlinked and overlapping phases: Airborne Paratrooper and glider-borne infantry drops (midnight to 0200 hours) with 23,000 troops descending behind the German lines on either flank, the US on the left or western flank and the British and Canadians on the right or eastern flank; from 0100 hours to 0400 hours activities to aid deception of the German forces to distract and create confusion. Even the false perception that another supposedly 'real' point of attack was occurring from Dover to the Pas-de-Calais; aerial bombardment (0300 hours) by Allied bombers against German coastal defences all along the northern French coast, the intensity of the bombardment to be agonising for the defenders; naval bombardment (0500 hours) – heavy salvos – from Allied naval ships standing off the Normandy shoreline covering the infantry approach to shore on landing craft; invasion (0600 to 0730 hours): the first waves of Allied infantry go ashore on five beaches codenamed Utah, Omaha, Gold, Juno and Sword over a fifty-mile stretch of coastline. Each to breach the defences, force their way inland to gain a lodgement in their immediate hinterlands – in order to join up in a consolidated bridgehead – then be prepared, on order and once reinforced, to advance towards Paris.

The planners, such as Irishman Commander Rickard Donovan, had achieved all of the pre-requisites for the attempted invasion being undertaken: the organisation of a colossal concentration of military assets to bring a massed fighting force to bear, focused at the one place and at the one time. This included air supremacy, allowing for a full umbrella of air cover over their lines of communication. The highly elaborate deception plan had achieved the element of surprise and they had assembled a gigantic armada of ships to get the invasion force across the English Channel, and an enormous number of landing craft to put the troops on shore, their ingenuity stretching as far as developing a range of specially modified armoured assault vehicles to negotiate the beach obstacles and, unimaginably, even two 'artificial ports', safe harbours to be brought with them and put in place where none existed before. They also designed 'PLUTO', the Pipeline under the Ocean, a petrol line to keep fuel flowing to aid the forward momentum of vehicles, both supply and fighting, to keep pace with the operation moving ahead. In all that and more the planners had succeeded in putting in place a uniquely remarkable achievement. It was now up to the infantry to secure the beaches and the fighting, due to the tides, started first on Utah and Omaha.

Fortunes of war, human frailty or a force of nature; for one, some or all of these reasons the Allied landings on Utah Beach occurred well over a mile west of the landing beach site selected. Chance had intervened and strong currents have been credited with sending the landing craft off course to a less heavily defended section of the beach.

Prior-planned and effective US paratrooper probing and persecution of inland German coastal defences, Allied with offshore naval shell fire, onshore shelling from the twenty-eight successfully landed DD tanks and the fervour of the fighting spirit of the troops going ashore – the 'fire in the belly' of the US infantrymen – saw them apply small-arms fire, grenades and even fire itself, more precisely the spraying of burning fuel from flamethrowers into bunkers, lead to a wilting of the German defences. Firefights erupted along the attacking front of the invaders, but the ferocity of the Allied assault caused the Germans to fall back towards their 'fortified farmhouses' and 'resistance points'. The retrograde nature of the retreat, trading space for time, still afforded them the advantage of fighting against infantry in the open, assaulting static, deliberate and prepared defences. Only the US 4th Infantry Division was wise to this ploy and called in close air support. The exchanges became those of Thunderbolt and Typhoon fighter bombers against 'resistance points'; flamethrowers against 'fortified farmhouses' and bazookas against bunkers. White-flamed phosphorous shells fired from the Thunderbolts caused burning incendiary material to flow on impact almost like a liquid, resulting in the incineration of occupant and ammunition alike. The burning to death of the Germans within the defensive positions was horrible, occasioning yet further retreat to the inland line of blockhouses, only for fighter bombers to again be favoured over ground attack. These destroyed the anti-tank guns, the heavy machine guns, the fortified defences and many of the weapon crews and riflemen within. The US infantry advanced to 'mop up' what remained.

The US 4th Infantry Division's assault on Utah Beach achieved a highly successful result. In all, 23,000 troops and some 1,700 vehicles landed on Utah, their vanguard penetrating four miles inland, making contact with the 101st Parachute Division, all for the loss of less than 200 casualties. 'Lightning Joe', Major General Joseph Lawton Collins, the Irish-American officer commanding US VII Corps, was delighted. So too was Major O'Malley, Second-in-Command 2nd Battalion 12th Infantry Regiment, and Second Lieutenant Preston Niland, 22nd Infantry Regiment, for they had survived D-Day. However, fate was not to be so kind to them over the next and coming days.

If all had gone well on Utah Beach on D-Day morning, the ongoing assault on Omaha was encountering a very different experience. The 'battle for the beaches' was about to take a 'bloody' turn.

8
OVERWROUGHT ON OMAHA

Soldiers in opposing armies do their best to defeat the enemy by whatever means possible; that is war, and alert and aware German shore defences were advantageous to good soldiers. Rommel was right: hold the Allies on the beaches and the invasion collapses. Pinned down with heavy casualties, Omaha Beach on D-Day was a blood bath. Landing on the beach without close support, deadly, intense, and sustained fire rained down unceasingly on the US infantrymen of the 1st and 29th Divisions.

For the German defenders of the 352nd Infantry Division, mostly 916th Grenadier Regiment, the early morning of 6 June (The Day of Days) was a shock. The time of waiting for the Allied enemy to arrive was suddenly over, and thrust into battle, the beach's tranquillity turned dramatically to turbulence, and serenity became a slaughterhouse. The German machine guns that criss-crossed rapid fire reaped a harrowing harvest. Before this day, every morning had seen the sea's regular rise and fall, the uniform horizon far-off. The tide calmly, peacefully ebbed and flowed in its self-same untroubled way, repeated and unchanging. This unvarying scenario, this constant sameness, was somehow irritating and irksome to the German defenders. For weeks they had waited and watched, drilled and rehearsed, while warning levels were raised then lowered, and tensions heightened then subsided. The levels of expectancy varied, fluctuating, alternating, but the sweeping panorama on which this played out remained unchanged and undisturbed.

The beach designated Omaha by the Allies was unlike Utah in that to the sides and rear of its three-mile stretch of semi-circular sandy beach, like the backdrop scenery of a stage setting, were high bluffs. More especially, at each end were broad, steep rocky cliffs. To the west, particularly Pointe du Hoc, was a prominent headland promontory and presumed location of 155 mm guns. All of this high ground gave the Germans an ideal line of sight onto the beach and equally a perfect line of fire onto anything approaching from the sea.

If Utah was a good beach to attack, Omaha was a good beach to defend, and the good fortune that greeted the Utah attackers was missing for the troops approaching Omaha. The pre-landing aerial bombardment had missed its intended targets and the naval salvo was ineffective; the former too wide of the mark, the latter, at only twenty minutes, too brief in duration. The Germans had made the most of the landscape's natural features, most especially along all the high ground and the cliffs, whereupon were placed an array of formidable gun emplacements housing 155 mm, 88 mm, 75 mm and 100 mm (Czech) guns, some fourteen in all. In addition, there were pillboxes (35), anti-tank guns (18) and machine-gun nests (85), all in a line of fortified strong points. Also different were the German soldiers themselves, well trained, more experienced and hard-bitten, with many snipers among them.

The lack of Allied close support was because the 'DD tanks' had been released too far out, in seas too rough for them. The blustery strong winds created swells and waves which battered the flotation devices, and only five of the thirty-four made it safely to shore. The twenty-nine that floundered sent their crews to a watery grave on the sea bed. Of the five tanks which made it to the beach, three arrived by landing craft, its ramp having initially malfunctioned. Notwithstanding, all five were shortly put out of action by mines and anti-tank fire and the infantry were on their own. The specialised obstacle-clearing AVRE, specially modified tanks designed by Major General Sir Percy Hobart, nicknamed 'Hobart's funnies' by the Americans, had been offered to US General Bradley by Montgomery, but except for the DD tanks and some armoured bulldozers, the latter had declined the offer. The landing had not begun well and its prospects were not improving.

Prepared, primed, well-drilled and rehearsed, the Germans on Omaha were meeting the potential Allied power and potency with vigour and violence, and more than matching their opposition. On Omaha, force met force. Both sides believed they were right and were committed to the fight. At stake was a foothold in Europe, to be gained or to be prevented. German toughness met American strength, and human beings were crushed in the collision. Among the first to die on Omaha was Joseph Flanagan, whose mother was from Clouna near Ennistymon in County Clare. Joseph was a US Ranger and the Rangers were in early, one Company assigned to the first wave of beach landings alongside A Company, 116th Infantry Regiment, and others given the objective of assaulting the battery of six 155 mm gun emplacements on Pointe du Hoc. But to fight there and on the beach at Omaha, Joseph Flanagan – among the first and subsequent waves of those thousands of US invaders – first had to be ferried there, and this task fell to the coxswains and crews of the landing craft.

William 'Bill' Dodds from Naas, County Kildare, joined the Royal Navy in 1935 as a boy sailor at the age of fourteen. He left Naas as there was no prospect of work, and in the 'hungry 1930s' the life of a sailor held a great attraction for him. Bill signed up for twelve years and trained at Davenport as a boy sailor. During the war he served on the Atlantic, Russian and Mediterranean convoys. His tour of duty also brought him to Omaha Beach during the D-Day landings. On the morning of 6 June 1944, Bill Dodds was serving on board the landing ship HMS *Empire Spearhead*, ferrying heavily laden troops from larger troop-carrying vessels, the soldiers disembarking precariously by climbing down 'scramble nets' strewn over the sides of the ship onto smaller landing craft bobbing underneath in the 'pitch and toss' of the undulating seas. They continued to 'run the gauntlet', first of heavy swells and the choppy sea as waves threatened to swamp the assault craft, and then from the distant fire of the German Coastal Battery artillery, this terror increasing and magnified by the additional fire from the Beach Batteries, mortars and machine guns the closer they got to shore. This 'exposure to risk' had to be repeated several times, and once ashore the hundreds of American infantrymen faced stiff German resistance. They were mowed down by machine-gun and sniper fire, blown to pieces by mines and mortars, or drowned before they ever got a chance to fire a shot: 'We could do nothing to help them,' was Bill Dodd's observation, frustration and regret clouding his voice as he recalled the carnage on what became known as 'Bloody Omaha'.

Meanwhile, David McCaughey from Dublin was among the Royal Navy crew aboard a larger LCT, and when his vessel was struck by a surface running torpedo he was forced to sail it back across the English Channel to safe harbour with its 'arse blown off'. An already memorable day; neither was his trip back uneventful. He was struck in the chest when they later came under 'friendly fire' from a US cruiser!

Michael d'Alton, from Dalkey, County Dublin, was a sub-lieutenant on LCT 796 at Omaha on D-Day. He had joined the Royal Navy because, 'I thought it was absolutely intolerable that Hitler was going to conquer Europe. I wanted to try and stop that awful German monster.' That morning, his landing craft beached on a shoreline obstacle, attached to which was a highly explosive Teller mine: 'The door was lowered onto a steel joust anti-invasion tripod with a Teller mine sitting on top. We should have been blown up. We backed away very, very carefully.' Dramatic as this near miss was, his abiding memory of the day was the tragic loss of an Allied tank crew, who disembarked from a nearby landing craft only to sink to the bottom of the sea on the edge of a large underwater hole. 'It was so simple and so quiet it has never left me; the awfulness of the quiet demise.' Michael d'Alton received the Legion d'Honneur with Chevalier from the French government on 26 January 2015. An extract from the official letter dated, 11 November 2014, from the French Ambassador to Ireland, reads: 'It is my privilege to inform you that by special Decree, Monsieur François Hollande, President of France, has knighted you as Chevalier de la Légion d'Honneur, the highest French honour.'

If the German shore defences were light and the defence weak on the section of the beach where the Allies made their fortuitous landing on Utah, there was no repeat of this charmed event on Omaha. Whatever foothold was to be gained, if indeed this was at all achievable, would have to be hard fought for. On Omaha, the German defences were dense, and the defenders deadly, disciplined and determined. The first US Infantry assault wave of seven landing craft with A Company, 116th Infantry, 29th Division on board were a thousand yards from the beach when Landing Craft No. 5 was struck by German Coastal Artillery and six men drowned. At 100 yards, Landing Craft No. 3 was hit; two soldiers were killed outright, a dozen men drowned. Five Landing Craft made it in and were greeted by a barrage of mortar fire before they even dropped their ramps. At 0636 hours, the five landing craft dropped their ramps. This was the signal for the Germans to sweep the line of landing craft with machine-gun fire from head on and both ends of the beach simultaneously. The bullets ripped into the first line of men before they even had time to put one foot forward, and others were cut down where they stood. Some managed to jump over the sides to avoid a similar fate, but dropping into water that was over their heads, and weighed down by overloaded backpacks and equipment, they drowned. Those that survived clutched to the sides of the landing craft, any semblance of orderly advance into the beach abruptly abandoned.

The sea along the shoreline began to run red with blood. Fear, desperation and shock gripped the Allied infantry as bullets continued to hit their targets, and the number of dead quickly mounted. Some of the wounded dragged themselves ashore, and on reaching the sands lay down exhausted, only for the incoming tide to drown them. For those who made it alive and unwounded to the shore, there was no cover to shield themselves against the incessant fire. The bare beach offered no protection; there were no shell holes, no bomb craters, no undulations of shingle and no sandbars. Nothing but the beach obstacles themselves and they were mostly some distance away. In all, Omaha was the invasion beach with the most distance to cover, some 450 yards from shoreline across exposed sand to the foot of the bluffs and high sand dunes. About half way up the beach were the majority of obstacles, and those who succeeded in reaching these found that they offered little protective cover, shelter or security from the unrestrained fire of the German machine gunners on the high ground.

The early stages of this decisive battle had all the hallmarks of a tragic failure. It was fast becoming costly to the courageous infantrymen without achieving any effect, and mere survival itself eluded most. Further waves of landing craft continued to be sent in, and many US soldiers were doomed to suffer the same fate as those gone before. Seawater-saturated radio sets failed, so there was both lack of contact and confused reporting, and it was only slowly that matters began to become apparent. Significantly, some of the smaller naval vessels standing off the shore became aware of the predicament and knew what needed to be done. On their own volition, without authority, they moved dangerously close to the coastline to give the desperately needed support fire. Disaster had visited the first wave, and those supposedly reinforcing them had to bail furiously with their helmets because of the rough seas to keep the second wave's (116th) six landing craft from swamping. On arrival to the shore, the occupants of the first landing craft shared the fate of their A Company comrades. Machine-gun bursts riddled bodies, others were equally hideously killed or wounded before ever reaching dry land, with exploding mortars adding to the shambles.

Frightened coxswains in the as yet uncommitted landing craft instinctively took evasive action and veered away from the chaos towards the right, heading in the direction of Pointe du Hoc. Meanwhile, other landing craft of the 116th Infantry Regiment continued on a direct course for a beach landing and ran into artillery fire. Direct hits were evident as their impact caused noticeable explosions, as ramps and other parts of the landing craft disintegrated in pieces. One, hit at the bow, began to sink with its stern lifted into the air, the men inside were tipped into the sea and drowned. Landing craft continued to be hit, some set on fire and others simply sank. In response, the 'maverick' Allied naval support ships 'lifted and shifted' their aim to counter-battery fire. This had the desired effect, and landing craft began to unload their human cargo, entering the water about chest height. The emerging troops mostly maintained their orderly formation, one behind the other, down the ramps as they had rehearsed on exercise. As the last man stepped off the landing craft, the crew hoisted the ramp and reversed rearwards in a disciplined and skilled manner as they had rehearsed on exercise. Above, the German machine gunners waited for the advancing US infantrymen to trudge slowly and deliberately into shallower water and, as they had rehearsed, when the water was at waist height on the invaders they opened fire. The fall of shot from the powerful MG 42 machine guns hit the men in front, the bullets passing through their bodies and hitting one, maybe even two or more soldiers behind.

Weighed down with heavy backpacks and equipment, staggering and stumbling through choppy water, and moving sluggishly at best, at close range the advancing infantry were easy targets for the Germans. Landing Craft Rockets (LCR) began firing salvos into the bluffs, making huge explosions but not necessarily proving accurate or effective. The German artillery opened up again and several more landing craft were sunk. Others, disabled and burning, collided with those both on their way in and out. The bodies of hundreds of dead US soldiers began rolling and swaying with the waves and the movement of the tide. These were added to as more waves of Allied landing craft came in and German machine-gun and mortar fire was unhesitatingly visited upon them. The sacrifice was huge, the slaughter significant and the carnage terrible. Two-thirds of the US infantry's first wave were estimated to have been casualties; in all it was calculated that more than 2,000 were killed.

Those who did make it to the foot of the sand dunes and bluffs were joined by others in subsequent waves once the ten or so destroyers, mixed British and American, combined concentrated fire directly on the German pillbox positions, strong points and 'resistance points'. As the well-aimed fire began to take good effect, tanks also began to get ashore in sufficient strength to provide the much-needed close support that had been lacking for so long. The Allies were slowly but steadily shooting themselves back into contention, and one among those now on shore was hugely relieved at this slow turning of events. Charles Durning, a private in the 386th Anti-Aircraft Battalion arriving in Normandy via Omaha Beach. Durning's father, an Irish immigrant, had joined the US Army in the First World War to gain his citizenship and lost a leg in that conflict. He died when Durning was only twelve years old from the effects of mustard gas. Durning was the only survivor of his unit that landed on Omaha Beach on D-Day, and in the process killed seven German gunners and suffered serious machine-gun wounds to his right leg. A week and a half later, on 15 June, Charles was wounded by a German 'Bouncing Betty' mine, a type of landmine that when triggered is launched into the air and detonates at about one metre from the ground, projecting a lethal spray of shrapnel in all directions. He survived his injuries, was discharged from military service in 1946, and after the war became a famous actor. He would later remark of his Normandy experience: 'There's not a day goes by I don't think about it. I can't talk about it. I don't even talk to my children about it. Certain things in our lives we can't share.' Gregory Muldoon, a 39-year-old painter from County Cavan, came ashore in the first wave at Omaha as a private in the 116th Infantry Regiment. Gregory Muldoon survived the horrors of D-Day only to fall in the fighting around Saint-Lô on 14 June, a week later.

With the infiltration of some US troops through a lesser-defended gap between Saint-Laurent and Colleville, a breakthrough on the beach looked possible. The turning point in the battle of Omaha Beach, from being close to the German defenders throwing the invaders back into the sea to a slow staged comeback, began. The beach-bound infantry and those already there benefitted from the pulverising of the pillboxes by the navy destroyers, some literally crushed to powder. Their fortunes were further reinforced by the arriving tanks, which maintained the momentum. Also, some armoured bulldozers came into play, and responding to this new set of circumstances the senior and junior on-ground leaders drove the understandably reluctant infantry forward. Smoke from grass fires, dust from explosions and the impaired vision of German machine gunners, now themselves under fire and grenade attack, all allowed groups of US infantry to reach the ravines through the bluffs and start to 'take out' individual machine-gun nests and progress laterally towards Vierville-sur-Mer. Ferocious close-in combat, hand to hand fighting with rifle butts and bayonets, and the use of flamethrowers was all part of the tough fighting that now took place, the Germans contesting throughout. American mortar fire from the beach began to come into play and this too had its effect. Resilience and the ability to readily recover from the shock of the near decimation of the first wave had allowed the Allies to pass through the trauma of the terrible circumstances in which they initially found themselves. Their resourcefulness, dogged determination and staying power in the face of abject adversity turned a wretched situation into a winnable one.

Concurrently, they also had to urgently address the scaling, assault and capture of the six 155 mm guns on the Pointe du Hoc. The Rangers had trained for the cliff attack on the Isle of Wight, under the direction of British commandos. Ten landing craft brought them ashore – one sank, and another was swamped – and at 1,000 yards out they came under fire from German mortars and machine guns. Despite this, the bulk of the force made it to the base of the cliff. Here, the distance from sea to shore was far less than on the beach, though the height of the cliff face was about thirty metres. Grapple hooks, ropes and rope ladders (even two London Fire Brigade ladders, which were too short in the event) were used to successfully scale the Pointe du Hoc. Fire support from the USS *Satterlee* and HMS *Talybont* ensured the

Germans on the cliff top were prevented from firing down on the Ranger assault force while they scaled the cliff face. However, stiff resistance was met and only half the force made it to the top. Securing a purchase on the Pointe du Hoc was difficult, but Ranger Force A succeeded in their mission.

Challenging and costly as the climb was, the situation took an unexpected turn when to their dismay the gun emplacements were found to be empty. It turned out that the guns had been removed for repair or to avoid destruction during the previous Allied aerial bombardments. Notwithstanding the shock of their absence, they were found nearby (700 metres away) and destroyed. On receipt of the 'success' signal, the firing of flares in the air, the plan had been for Ranger reinforcements (5th Ranger Battalion and two companies of 2nd Ranger Battalion), to join them on Pointe du Hoc to consolidate the capture of the high ground. In the event of no signal being fired in time (taken to mean the assault was unsuccessful) then the second Ranger force were instead to proceed to join the main body of the attack on the beach. The signal was fired, but it was delayed because of the time taken to find the guns, by which time the alternative option had already been chosen. This was significant, because now 'Ranger Force A' on the cliff top were without reinforcements and running out of ammunition. No further exploitation of their success could be attempted, indeed they would be lucky to keep what they had gained. In the face of several German counter-attacks, the costliest chapter of the battle for Pointe du Hoc was yet to unfold. Yet the defence of the vital (high) ground gained was crucial.

It had been a long and costly six hours, but the build-up of US forces landing on the beach became apparent, and just after midday nearly 20,000 troops and associated vehicles with assorted supplies were being landed. They had landed on the beach, gained a tenuous 'toehold', rather than a foothold, and fighting to force a proper lodgement was ongoing. D-Day on Omaha was bloody; success was limited and the outcome was still not fully certain. It would take further fighting to achieve the Allies' aims.

A stark scene was to be forever seared into the memory of Dubliner Michael d'Alton. During the days following D-Day, Sub-Lieutenant Michael d'Alton and his landing craft crew were to make a number of repeat journeys across the English Channel to and from Omaha Beach, ferrying much needed supplies to the Allies consolidating their bridgehead. Two weeks after the (Landings) day it was a bank holiday for the villagers. Local children were playing on the beach, now safely and securely in Allied hands and cleared of obstacles and mines, and he watched as a 'kick about' with a soccer ball was in progress:

> I remember one little thing, there was a fellow dribbling a football, a soccer ball, along the wet beach. The tide was out and he dribbled it into what looked like a pool. It was actually one of these little hollow scoops from the propeller of a previous landing craft, because they would have to keep those running to try and keep themselves square. Well, the ball went into the pool, and so did he. And the next thing there was a damn great explosion. And the football came out in bits and he came out in bits, and that was that, rather sobered me up. The feeling was less like a bank holiday then.

In August 2017, Michael d'Alton's daughter, Sonda, and his son, Mark, felt it fitting and entirely appropriate to spread a portion of his ashes in the sea offshore of Omaha Beach, with the help of the local lifeboat crew, at the approximate location of his approach to the beach, given his D-Day experiences were such a marked, deep and important facet throughout his life.

9

DEFENDING DEMOCRACY ON GOLD BEACH

Built in the 1620s for the homesick Marie de' Medici, widow of Henry IV, the Italianate style of the Palais du Luxembourg in Paris' 6th Arrondissement was intended to remind her of the Pitti Palace in her native Florence. The gardens were part formal, with terraces and mature trees, a large fountain in the centre and all throughout it was crowded with sculptures. The Palace had been passed on to various royals until the Révolutionnaires converted it into a prison, increased the size of the garden, and made it a public institution. Today the Palais du Luxembourg hosts the French Senate, the upper house of the French government.

On the arrival of the Germans to France in 1940, the Luftwaffe (German Air Force) made it their headquarters. After 1942, however, the Luftwaffe was in decline, with its strength sapped, its units under strength, and crews and pilots overstretched. To keep a fighter aircraft in the air, active and fighting, required spare parts, coolant, lubricants and oil, and in 1944 these were in short supply. There was also simply insufficient aircraft and not enough fresh pilots. This was in stark contrast to the Allied air fleet. Before seven in the morning on D-Day, only three Luftwaffe night fighters had flown over the Normandy beaches. After that German pilots sat in the cockpits of their Messerschmitt 109 fighters and waited, but no order came. Luftwaffe HQ did send up reconnaissance planes to look for the 'fake fleet' off Dieppe, chasing the diversionary window of chaff to no avail. At 9 am they issued orders for aircraft to head for the coast and concentrate on the troop transports and bombers, but rescinded these almost immediately. Luftwaffe HQ in Paris had considered the prevailing weather conditions as unlikely to present a favourable opportunity for invasion and were caught napping. It was difficult now to make sense of the situation and it was not a straightforward decision as to where to send those fighters that were left, the bulk having been moved nearer to Germany. This situation led to them issuing contradictory orders for a number of hours.

Mid-morning on D-Day, a 'recce' flight of three Messerschmitt 109s were ordered from an airfield in the Évreux-Lisieux sector to fly to the nearby coast (west of Caen, over Gold and Juno beaches). Flying at speeds in excess of 500 kph and at height, the Normandy coastline was not long in coming into view and the sight that greeted them astonished the pilots. If a description was possible, relating it was beyond imagination. An indescribable number of ships floated offshore, and the beaches were crammed with vehicles waiting to move off as enormous resources were brought to bear on the sands. Ahead of them, the Allies were fiercely fighting to advance inland, and there was also ample evidence of the beach battles still in progress. Smoke, flames, explosions, vehicles and landing craft on fire were visible, and muzzle flashes from artillery, bomb impacts inland and not least the concentric shock waves from naval salvos were noticeable on the flooded plains.

Only one of the three Messerschmitt 109s of the recce flight landed safely back to Évreux-Lisieux airfield. In all, less than 100 German fighters took to the skies on D-Day, and even then belatedly. Luftwaffe HQ had difficulty coming to terms with the confused happenings in Normandy, and the hallways and rooms of the Palais du Luxembourg were full of uncertain and indecisive Luftwaffe HQ personnel. The scale of D-Day was beyond German imagination; it had literally to be seen to be believed. There had been nothing like it in magnitude, scope or the sheer extent of its dimensions ever before. A major landing on beaches was completely unexpected. It was not thought possible in the first instance, and all the more because of all the beach obstacles and coastal fortifications that had been constructed on and along them.

Gold Beach lay between Le Hamel and La Rivière on the coast and Bayeux inland. Famous for its tapestry – a relic depicting the landing of the French Duke William the Conqueror in England in 1066, nine centuries previously – Bayeux was significant in the invasion plan as its capture would make it difficult for the Germans to move in reinforcements. If there were differences between the events on Omaha compared to Utah, there were distinct dissimilarities again about what transpired on Gold Beach. Firstly, this was a British Army objective; secondly, the full range of strange and specialised contraptions – the modified armoured assault vehicles of the 79th Armoured Division (Hobart's Funnies) – were brought into play; thirdly, the defenders were able to avail themselves of the beachfront buildings they had converted into 'fortified resort towns'. By strengthening the many outlying seafront villas, complemented with the building of amply sized and multiple strong points, this rendered the charming seaside towns into well-defended, up front entrenchments. Finally, as the D-Day assault was being made on a flooding tide, the physical beach space would be much smaller, coinciding with the 'hoped-for' arrival of increasing numbers of troops, tanks, vehicles and supplies. However, should the German defence not be breached, the build-up on the foreshore with the tide pressing on their backs would make the tightly packed Allied troops an all too tempting and unmissable target for German artillery.

In the first instance, way down at the tactical level, D-Day was a very personal experience for the individual soldier. The exposure to danger was a frightening sensation, and this trepidation for many began with the descent over the side of the troop-carrying ship to the landing craft below. Most likely 'fortified' by a tot of Navy rum, the transfer process for each soldier involved physically having to move, but also having to make a psychological shift to change his mental state to accommodate a far more heightened sense of the dangerous situation. Consciously aware of his vulnerability, his circumstances becoming more hazardous to reach the 'floating shoebox' (the landing craft) below involved having to climb down the ship's side on a 'scramble net', a large net hung over the side of the ship on which he had to find his footing and grip. A firm hold on the rungs of the netting was difficult to achieve as the rope was coarse and thick and hung flush against the ship's hard hull. There was barely sufficient space to place the toe of one's boot onto the crosspiece of the netting and wrap cold fingers fully around the rope. To add to this predicament, the motion of the ship, the steepness and height to descend, the weight of a heavy backpack and equipment and the bobbing up and down of the landing craft in the heavy swell below – into which he had to accurately jump and not into the sea – took sharp focus, drawing on reserves of concentration and courage to execute accurately. When fully loaded, the landing craft moved away from the ship, shore bound, only to meet further adversity. They were being dispatched into danger, many to death itself.

The danger became increasingly evident by the mortar and shell fire ranged against them the nearer they got to the shore, magnified enormously when the ramp came down at the bow of the 'boat' as the landing craft's shallow hull scraped the beach. Coming under fire is a chastening experience, because there is a sudden and sharp realisation that someone is actually trying to kill you. The firer's intent is to end your life, with bullets and projectiles designed to rupture as much 'critical' body tissue and vital organs as possible. This is a harsh reality, the reaction to which causes fear and outrage, feelings of shock and anger, rage and resentment, all at once. In the moment, felt uppermost is one's mortality; you are conspicuously conscious of the closeness of death, the proximity of peril, and the close quarters of a possible calamitous end. The experience is frightening, but the soldiers were well trained to combat that experience.

One of those so trained, landing on Gold Beach, was Joseph 'Joner' Mullally (28) from Moate, County Westmeath, a private in the Green Howards. A labourer and former soldier in the Irish Army, 'Joner' found himself going ashore in the company of Company Sergeant-Major Stanley Hollis. On arrival they found Gold Beach in a state of organised chaos: tanks, jeeps, vehicles of every type had been hit and knocked out of action, some on fire. The grass just off the beach was burning and clouds of smoke obscured a view of what lay beyond. Wounded men (some Germans among them) were sitting at the top of the beach and stretcher bearers were carrying others down to the landing craft from where 'Joner' and the sergeant-major had landed. Shells and mortar bombs were falling about them, so Private Mullally and Company Sergeant-Major Hollis ran to the top of the beach and along its ridge. There they found coils of barbed wire and, amazingly, amid the very heavy barrage of German artillery and support weapon fire, some unruffled sea birds sitting nonchalantly in front of them, calm and casual among the confusion and commotion. Taking in the scene, Private

Mullally remarked to Company Sergeant-Major Hollis, 'No bloody wonder they are there Sergeant-Major (with so many shells and mortars being fired), there's no room in the air for them!' Moving on down the coastal town's esplanade, MG 34 machine-gun fire was opened up on them out of a concrete slit embrasure from a well camouflaged pillbox and Private Joseph Mullally's war was suddenly over, his life abruptly ended. He was buried in Bayeux War Cemetery.

The British troops' ability to get off the beach had been severely contested by the Germans for some time, their beach obstacles had struck some of the landing craft causing them to sink or catch fire, the flames engulfing some of those on board. German 88 mm guns opened up at the landing craft on to the beach's shoreline as they lowered their ramps. Effective bursts of machine-gun fire targeted the British infantry exiting the landing craft and scrambling up the beach. In reply, British naval guns began zeroing in on the German 88 mm gun emplacements, scoring direct hits and otherwise disabling them, putting some out of action. The British had also brought their armour ashore with the infantry, so close support was at hand. So too, importantly, were the obstacle-clearing AVREs, which played a vital part in tackling the impediments to movement just as they had been designed to. The DD tanks ploughed ashore with the infantry, but on Gold Beach the 'Petard' tanks especially made an enormous contribution, their heavy guns blasting through the concrete sea wall and pillboxes, allowing the infantry to pile through and advance. Advance too did the 'crab' tanks, their huge flails beating paths through minefields for other tanks and infantry to follow.

Mines and anti-tank fire, along with armour piercing shells, accounted for a number of the AVREs, and turrets and tracks blown off, the ammunition inside exploding, wrecked tank hulls littered the beach. At times it appeared as if individual duels were taking place between tank and gun emplacements, often the outcome decided on whichever crew could bring the most effective fire to bear first. Sometimes split seconds were the difference between survival and death. Close air support, especially the Allied 'umbrella' of fighter bomber aircraft, was crucial, and their involvement contributed greatly in helping the British infantry ashore and keeping it moving inland on D-Day.

Regimental Sergeant-Major Sean O'Donovan (Drumcondra, Co. Dublin), Royal Artillery. He escaped from a number of prisoner of war camps and also fought alongside Italian and Russian partisan resistance groups. (Courtesy of his nephew Lieutenant-Colonel Fred O'Donovan)

Sub-Lieutenant Michael d'Alton (Dalkey, Co. Dublin), Royal Navy, was the Landing Craft Commander at Omaha Beach on D-Day. He was involved in many supply trips back and forth across the English Channel thereafter. (Courtesy of his daughter Sonda d'Alton)

RAF Dakota aircraft kicked off the D-Day invasion of Nazi-occupied Europe by dropping paratroops early on 6 June 1944. (Gary Eason/Flight Artworks/Alamy Stock Photo)

Dr Richard J. Hayes (west Limerick), Director of the National Library and the chief cryptographer with Irish Defence Forces' 'G2' intelligence section, was successful in cracking the 'Goertz Cipher'. (Courtesy of the National Library of Ireland)

J.S. (Josh) Honan (Co. Clare), member of the 7th Cadet Class at the Military College, Curragh Camp, Co. Kildare, later joined the Royal Engineers and was attached to the 5th Canadian Assault Engineers on Juno Beach on D-Day. (Courtesy of the editor of *An Cosantóir*)

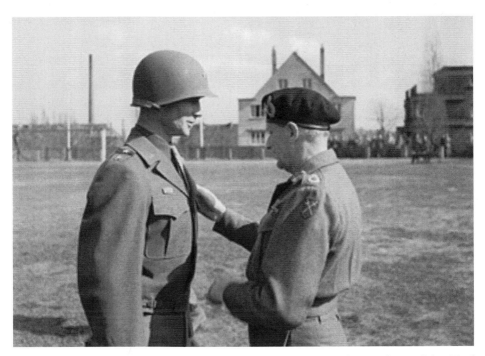

General 'Jumpin' Jim' James Gavin (of Irish parents), Commanding Officer of the 82nd US Airborne Division. At thirty-seven years old, he was the youngest Major General to command an US army division. He was to complete four combat jumps – including D-Day – during the war. Here he is being presented with a medal decoration by Field Marshal Bernard Law Montgomery ('Monty'), whose family has long and deep roots in Co. Donegal. (Courtesy of the Imperial War Museum)

Search Officer Fred O'Donovan (Drumcondra, Co. Dublin), member of the RAF Missing Research and Enquiry Service (1944–53), and the brother of Sean O'Donovan. (Courtesy of his son Lieutenant-Colonel Fred O'Donovan)

Sergeant Patrick 'Paddy' Gillen (Galway), 1st Special Services Brigade ('Commandos'), came ashore at Sword Beach on D-Day, connected up with the 7th Parachute Regiment which, in turn, reinforced the glider-borne 'Ox and Bucks' (of whom 10 per cent were Irish), famously known for securing Pegasus Bridge. Paddy Gillen and his unit 'dug in' and held vital high ground on the west flank of the invasion area for forty-two days. (Courtesy of his son Robin Gillen)

USAAF Captain Patrick James Ness, US 81st Fighter Squadron (his mother was Irish, a McAuliffe), flew four sorties on D-Day. (Courtesy of his son Phillip Ness)

Captain Patrick James Ness of Michigan, whose mother was Irish (a McAuliffe), flew four sorties over Normandy on D-Day in his P-47 Thunderbolt ('the Jug') with the US 81st Fighter Squadron. The 'P' in P-47 stands for pursuit, and the sorties over Normandy on 6 June saw him in pursuit of both 'directed' and 'opportunity' targets. His initial memory of the day was to have been woken up early to discover that while they (the pilots) were sleeping, their fighter bomber aircraft had been painted overnight with the black and white striped identification markings unique to D-Day, 'in poor quality paint, more like whitewash.' They had come over from America in February 1944 and flew their first operational missions commencing 1 May out of Leamington airfield. His father, a Norwegian immigrant who arrived to the US in 1872, was a mining engineer and so he gravitated towards that industry, which happened to have a large Irish involvement associated with it. It has been said of the immigrant Irish that for those 'Americans' already there they built their bridges and their railroads, policed their streets, fought their fires and their wars. The term 'sand hogs' was sometimes used to describe those involved in bridge building, while the term 'gandy dancers' was applied to the railroad workers, a reference to the straight-armed style of Irish dancing. After eleven years in New York he went to Michigan and became involved in the Ancient Order of Hibernians (AOH), an Irish-American society that brought him into contact with his soon-to-be 'Irish' wife, to whom Patrick James was subsequently born.

When the Second World War broke out, Patrick joined the 81st Fighter Squadron and so followed his subsequent D-Day involvement. On 25 June, nearly three weeks after D-Day, the squadron left Leamington airfield in England and was relocated to Advanced Landing Ground (A-17), an airfield in Normandy which had runways of pierced steel matting laid over the ground. He and his 'wing man' were given a 'Paris Pass' and were set up on a double blind date, but he made a connection with his wing man's partner and they were to subsequently marry on 10 June 1945 in St Patrick's Chapel in the Irish College at 5 Rue des Irlandais in Paris (5th Arrondissement). His bride was Olivia Marie De Luco, who herself had Irish blood – her maternal grandmother was a Campbell O'Brien. She had been sixteen when the Germans 'goose stepped' into Paris, and she became a member of the French Resistance and later the Free French Forces.

For his part, Patrick James Ness was to find himself in 'US Air Force Intelligence', loaned (seconded) to the OSS, and was involved after Victory in Europe (VE) Day, 8 May 1945, in seeking out German scientists and sending them to the United States to work on 'military projects'. In all he saw service from 1942 to 1968, fought in three 'hot' wars (the Second World War, Korean and Vietnam wars) and at the height of the 'Cold War' flew a B-47 bomber for Strategic Air Command. His mantra throughout his service was 'You do not volunteer for anything, you do not turn anything down.'

Private John Keating, from County Wexford, 1st Battalion, Hampshire Regiment, came ashore at Gold Beach on D-Day. He had joined the British Army in November 1943, having previously served in the Irish Army. D-Day 6 June 1944 was Private Keating's first time under fire, and a memorable baptism it was. Now 'inescapably in action', he found himself in the thick of the fighting. The Hampshire Regiment fought through the beachfront battlefield, progressed the assault and secured their objective. Moving inland off the beach, he fought alongside his comrades into the *bocage* countryside for the next fortnight until 19 June. He was among the battalion's heavy casualties as they attacked Hottot. He was buried at Bayeux War Cemetery.

La Rivière secured, La Hamel was still in German hands along the beachfront. However, a sufficient advance through to Bayeux had been secured by the British 50th Division, so this was progressed with, as was the beach obstacle and minefield clearance activity. The follow-on brigades came ashore and kept up the momentum, expanding the bridgehead towards Bayeux and occupying the coast, linking up with the US troops arriving from Omaha. La Hamel was subsequently captured in the use of the reverse sequence, which occurred further east on Gold Beach this time, the 'Funnies' again playing their part. A flail tank ('Crab') managed to mount the sea wall and beat a path across the minefield. This allowed the infantry to pour through, supported by 'Petard' tanks with their concrete-busting flying dustbin bombs.

About 1,000 casualties, killed, wounded and missing, were recorded by the British 50th Division on Gold Beach. The resourceful deployment and determination of the Assault Vehicles Royal Engineers from the 79th Armoured Division saw such a successful breach through the Atlantic Wall that Bayeux was occupied intact. So too was the taking of Arromanches, vital for the establishing of Mulberry 'B', the artificial harbour with its floating causeways and pier head, the 'harbour' having a total area the size of Dover Port.

Cork man Sean Walsh (British Merchant Navy) had a unique view of D-Day. Unexpectedly, he found himself trapped alone on a deliberately sunken ship as the invasion began. He had been on a ship that had left the English coast on 5 June as part of a single file convoy on a vital mission. Once the vessels reached the beaches of Arromanches-les-Bains, the crews were instructed to purposefully sink them by blowing holes in their hulls. This controlled sinking allowed the ship's hulls to settle onto the sand in the shallow sea, acting as a breakwater and calming the waves for the soon to be arriving soldiers, and not long after the component parts of Mulberry 'B' were to be assembled in situ. Only matters took a bizarre twist for Sean Walsh, as having gone to bed in his half-submerged ship along with the rest of the crew, he awoke the following morning alone. He discovered that all of his shipmates had left; Sean had quite literally missed the boat and was stranded alone at sea as the largest amphibious armada in history began to disgorge its occupants and the invasion of the Normandy beaches began to unfold.

With a vivid view of the ongoing action he recalled seeing Allied soldiers jumping from their landing craft, many falling to their deaths in the sea. Interviewed in the Cork *Holly Bough* at Christmas 2015, Walsh, then ninety-three, stated: 'I never thought that I was going to die', adding of his shipmates and superiors, 'I did not want to bother them; there was a war going on. I knew what they were doing and that they would send someone as soon as they could.' The beach he could see, Arromanches, was to be the location for the installation of the Mulberry Harbour 'B', allowing the Allies to supply its precious foothold on the French coast as they advanced inland. Sean Walsh spent ten days alone on the ship, and the Morse code he learned at the 'Wireless School' served him well as he kept contact with his colleagues, signalling by flashlight. Content that his colleagues knew of his location and situation he remained calm, sustained by the plenty of food on board.

From the Blackrock family of a well-established Cork businessman who ran several pubs around the city, on the outbreak of war Sean completed his course at the Radio Officers' Association training school in Tivoli, Cork, where he studied with many people from Cork who later lost their lives in the war. He began his Merchant Navy career in Liverpool, where he was assigned to the MV *Portfield*, a 10,000-tonne tanker. Shortly after, he and his shipmates embarked on a perilous mission to lure the German battle fleet out of the Norwegian fjords so that their Royal Navy colleagues could attack them in open sea. The German ships took the bait and six destroyers attacked the convoy in December 1941, and in turn were attacked by the Royal Navy. A few weeks later, when his ship was at anchor, a lone German plane appeared out of the sky, hitting the ship tied up alongside his. Four people were killed and six badly injured. He recalls:

> I came out of my cabin and there was a plane flying low, touching the mountains. I watched him coming over; the bomb dropped and hit the ship next to me, which sank. It did not hit us. The bomb exploded and I got a bit of shrapnel in my leg. I was bleeding a lot. That was the only injury I got during the war. I pulled a bit of it out. I could walk.

After his D-Day misadventure, Sean Walsh worked on ships that carried machinery for rebuilding and went to China, Japan, Singapore, Iceland, Venezuela, Jamaica, the US, Canada and throughout Europe. He left the Merchant Navy in late 1946, married his Cork sweetheart, and having spent a few years in England, departed to Canada in 1950. His credentials earned at Wireless Radio College and his wartime experience saw him hired by the Canadian National Telegraph service. In 2015, Sean was awarded the Legion d'Honneur in France for his efforts in 'securing the deliverance of France'.

Fellow Corkonian James Downey from Old Head, Kinsale, was also on the seas off Normandy on D-Day. A member of the Royal Navy and former farmer, he had gone to England because of the Depression in Ireland due to the 'Economic War' and Ireland's refusal to pay land annuities and was called up.

John Hyland from Waterford, and formerly Irish Defence Forces, 6th Battalion, Duke of Wellington's Regiment, landed in Normandy in the follow up waves of reinforcements on 11 June and found himself in action within twenty-four hours. One week later on 20 June he was among the casualties (over twenty officers and 360 other ranks) suffered by his Battalion killed and wounded. Unfortunately, John Hyland was among the former, those fatally injured.

Joseph Mulcahy from County Westmeath, John Keating from County Wexford and John Hyland lie among the over 4,000 (4,144) tidy, carefully looked-after graves in Bayeux War Cemetery. They at least were known to their families, their burial places marked and named. 'Known unto God' is inscribed on a memorial recording the names of another 1,800 soldiers whose bodies were never found. They fought and died on D-Day and in Normandy for the freedoms and rights we all enjoy today. Freedoms and rights earned by the service and sacrifice of the Irish who joined the Allied struggle.

At its peak during the Second World War, the Irish Defence Forces had some 42,000 serving personnel. During that time, 4,983 soldiers deserted from the Irish Defence Forces to join the Allied armies fighting Germany and Japan. In mid-June 2012, the Irish Minister for Defence, Alan Shatter TD, in a statement to the Dáil (Irish Parliament), announced there would be a pardon and amnesty for soldiers who deserted the Irish Army to fight for the Allies. The Minister said that in addressing the question of desertion during this period, the government acknowledged the Second World War gave rise to circumstances that were grave and exceptional, that no distinction was made between those who fought on the Allied side for freedom and democracy and those who absented themselves for other reasons. The Minister, on behalf of the Irish government, apologised for the manner in which these soldiers were treated after the war by the State. At the time of his announcement, it was estimated that 100 'deserters' were still alive. The 2012 announcement in the Dáil recognised 'the value and importance of their military contribution to the Allied victory' and that the introduction of the legislation 'would grant a pardon and amnesty to those who absented themselves from the Irish Defence Forces without leave or permission to fight on the Allied side'. He continued:

> The Government recognises the value and importance to the State of the essential service given by all those who served in the [Irish] Defence Forces throughout the period of [the Second World War]. It is essential to the national interest that members of the Defence Forces do not abandon their duties at any time, especially at a time of crisis, and no responsible Government could ever depart from this principle.

He noted that in August 1945, the government issued an Emergency Powers Order, and summarily dismissing the 'deserters' from the Defence Forces and disqualified them for seven years from holding employment or office remunerated from the State's Central Fund. He also noted that individuals were not given a chance to explain their absence, and 'No distinction was made between those who fought on the Allied side for freedom and democracy and those who absented themselves for other reasons'. Members of the Irish Defence Forces left their posts at that time to fight on the Allied side against tyranny and, together with many thousands of other Irish men and women, played an important role in defending freedom and democracy. Those who fought on the Allied side also contributed to protecting the State's sovereignty and independence. The Minister went on to say:

> In the time since the outbreak of the Second World War our understanding of history has matured, we can re-evaluate actions taken long ago, free from the constraints that bound those directly involved and without questioning or revisiting their motivations. It is time for understanding and forgiveness. At a time of greater understanding of the shared history and experiences of Ireland and Britain, it is right that the role played by Irish veterans who fought on the Allied side be recognised and the rejection they experienced be understood. To that end, this Government has now resolved to provide a legal mechanism that will provide an amnesty to those who absented themselves from our Defence Forces and fought with the Allied Forces in World War

II and to provide a pardon to those who were individually court-martialled. This will be achieved without undermining the general principle regarding desertion. The proposed legislation, which I intend to introduce later this year, will provide that the pardon and amnesty does not give rise to any right or entitlement or to any liability on the part of the State.

However, the Minister emphasised the government did not condone desertion and 'fully recognises, values and respects the contribution of all those who stood by their post with the Irish Defence Forces'.

10
JELLYFISH

For the troops wading ashore and those already on the beaches, fear was inescapable. Theirs was a helpless sense of defencelessness and counter-intuitive reasoning for their security; they had to keep moving quickly, regardless of losses. Outrunning the aim of the German gunners above them was their only means of survival because that was the nature of this combat. In ground combat you can stay where you are and be terrified and die, or you can stare down fear and move. Theirs was a vulnerability that was only overcome by taking chances. The barrage of orchestrated violence overtook their senses. They could 'see' the explosions, feel their heat, power and shock waves and hear their 'loudness'. The deafening booms were punctuated by the racket of rocket, mortar, machine-gun and small-arms fire.

They were in the enemy's prepared 'killing ground' and were now mercilessly being 'zeroed-in' upon. They responded with flamethrowers, grenades, bangalores, bullets and bayonets. Cruelty was met by ferociousness, viciousness by ruthlessness. The close-quarter fighting was wild, untamed and predatory. There was killing, wounding and near misses too, in ugly, horrible, chaotic scenes of inhumanity. Opportunities were clutched at wherever they appeared, it was as much instinct and improvisation as it was training that was relied on as matters turned out not quite right; when the intimidating, uncomfortable reality, the panicked, pressurised actuality, became what it terrifyingly was – kill or be killed.

Burning out or blowing up the beach bunkers the Allied troops moved on, maintaining their momentum inland to meet the next line of defences.

With reinforced vigour, reinforcements and close air support they attacked the fall-back resistance points. Tanks too, Shermans and Churchills, took their toll on these trenches with their 'Tobruk' type installations. The Churchill 'Crocodile' was a large, mobile flamethrower on tracks and was horribly deadly.

★★★

'Swordfish', 'Goldfish' and 'Jellyfish', abbreviated to 'Sword', 'Gold' and 'Jelly', were the names of the beaches to be assaulted by the British and Canadian forces. Churchill, the British Prime Minister, objected to the idea that soldiers were bound to die on a beach codenamed 'Jelly' and insisted on the change to 'Juno'. Whatever it was called, the beach and the German defences on it had to be attacked and taken in order for the objectives of the Canadian 3rd Division to be achieved. The Canadians would have the support of British units, the 8th Battalion of the King's Liverpool (Irish) Regiment among them, and the capture of high ground west of Caen (including Carpiquet Airport); the Bayeux–Caen railway line and the seaside towns of Courseulles, Bernières, Saint-Aubin and Graye-sur-Mer were the main objectives. These towns were immediately adjacent to the beach, so once safely across the sands it was straight into street fighting. Fighting in built up areas requires 'extra', 'additional' and 'more' of everything: training, troops, time, ammunition and casualties.

In August 1942, the Canadians, with British support, had previously been involved in Operation Jubilee, the disastrously abortive landing raid at the French port of Dieppe. Designed to test the feasibility of a cross Channel invasion, the raid had not benefitted from well-considered planning and ended in abject failure, with 4,963 killed, wounded or captured. This Allied failure had been seized upon by Joseph Goebbels, Propaganda Minister for the Third Reich:

We have fortified the coast of Europe from northern Norway to the Mediterranean and it is armed with the most implacable weapons the 20th century has to offer. This is why an enemy attack, however powerful and furious it may be, is doomed to failure. At Dieppe they only lasted nine hours and that was before the wall was built. If they last nine hours next time, they will be doing well.

Two years later the Canadians were back and they were not alone. The fury and power the Allies brought with them was unimagined. That said, the preliminary naval and aerial bombardments to soften up the beach defences and destroy coastal strong points on Juno Beach were less effective than hoped. The rough weather also created difficulties and delays, which meant the landing craft arrived on a higher tide than hoped and became more susceptible to the now submerged mined beach obstacles. Matters were further compounded by encountering heavy German resistance. Landing craft suffered heavy casualties before they ever reached or got clear of the beach.

Invaluable experience in amphibious assaults and inland fighting had been gained by previous Allied invasions, particularly Sicily in July 1943 and Salerno (Italy) in September the same year. Lessons learned from Dieppe, North Africa (Morocco), Sicily and Salerno were identified, analysed and applied to the planning of the 6 June 1944 invasion of France. All this harsh experience and the hard lessons coalesced for Operation Overlord. There were many associated studies, additional taskings and affiliated operations connected to Operation Overlord. One such supporting D-Day operation was Tarbrush, put into effect from July 1943 into early 1944. This was a series of covert missions carried out by, among others, 3 Troop (Group X) 10 Commando, conducting hazardous, audacious night-time raids on the coast of northern France. Sand samples from beaches, specimens of the beach obstacles, photographs, even prisoners for interrogation were taken. Later, and away from the Normandy beaches in mid-May 1944, 10 Commando undertook other raids to aid the deception plan.

A successful surprise invasion also required total air superiority over the English Channel and Normandy. In the months preceding D-Day, Allied bomber aircraft (with fighter support) were diverted from their prior mission of targeting the German Rhine–Ruhr industrial heartland of military hardware and munitions manufacturing to aerial attacks on airfields, radar and defence installations instead, but especially transport routes: roads, bridges and railway lines, stations and shuttle yards, plus aircraft manufacturing facilities in particular. All this multiple bombing activity had its associated risk, and such perilous pursuit saw many Allied bombers shot down and air crews lost (killed and captured). Wounded among them was Fred O'Donovan from Drumcondra, Dublin, a member of the RAF who served as a Wireless Operator/Air Gunner-Top Turret (WOP/AG) on a Lancaster bomber. His wounds, however, were received as a result of 'friendly fire' – he was hit by shrapnel in the knee when a nearby USAF crew 'cleared their guns' into his aircraft.

Sent to Long Kesh, Northern Ireland (then a military hospital) on recuperation he volunteered for a new unit, the RAF Missing Research and Enquiry Service (MRES, 1944–52). Established in 1944 to trace the 42,000 RAF personnel who were listed as 'missing believed killed', the MRES was highly successful, and in 1945 was expanded to cope with demand. Without the benefits modern technology offers, just a strong desire to bring home those who had not returned, the MRES was able to account for over two-thirds of the missing personnel, who were identified and reinterred in Commonwealth War Graves Commission plots. Their work allowed families the comfort of knowing what had happened to their loved ones and the location of their final resting place, and as such afforded them the dignity to finally grieve. Fred O'Donovan recalls, 'It was the best, most fulfilling and honourable thing I did in my entire life. I felt what I was doing was something so right, as it was so important for the families of those RAF men missing since as far back as even Dunkirk'.

Fred O'Donovan joined the RAF because he believed he was 'defending Ireland', that 'Hitler was a world problem' so he 'wanted to fight'. An excellent soccer player, he was picked for the RAF XIs, representing them throughout Europe. A scout approached him at one of the matches and he was subsequently selected for Arsenal – the very same day he was told he had TB. As an RAF MRES search officer, Fred O'Donovan was, post-invasion, despatched to places throughout France and Belgium where aircraft were believed to have crashed. This work involved on ground investigation interviewing local town mayors, gendarmerie, priests and anyone else likely to have had any morsel of information that would help. Identification of airmen who had died was often assisted by the smallest of details, initials on a personal artefact, if lucky a serial number, or maybe a name on a laundry label on clothing. Painstaking, often harrowing, it was nonetheless richly rewarding work. It even had its surprises; one day finding a 'live body', so to speak, a 'downed airman' still alive and well and very happy in his circumstance.

Seeking assistance one day in the newly established Irish Red Cross Hospital at Saint-Lô, Fred O'Donovan met who he believed was the caretaker, an Irishman named Sam, with whom he had a pleasant chat. Thinking no more of it, some months later he was requested to attend a function in the British Embassy in Paris, as being Irish himself he might assist the Embassy staff playing host to an invited guest, an Irish writer whom they regarded as rather shy, reticent and quiet spoken. When he was subsequently introduced to the writer, a Mr Samuel Beckett, Fred O'Donovan immediately recognised him as the 'caretaker' he had met some months beforehand at the Irish Red Cross Hospital at Saint-Lô.

He was also involved in the investigation of the search for the bodies of the '50', those escapees from the Allied Airforce personnel prisoner of war camp at Stalag Luft III in Sagan, Poland, which was later the subject of the 1963 epic Hollywood film, *The Great Escape*. It was somewhat coincidental that his work brought him into the search for the dead aircrew escapees, so to speak, because although not one of the '50', his very own brother Sean, also in the British Army, was a bit of an escape artist himself. Taking his father's bike in Dublin, he cycled all the way to Belfast and joined the Royal Artillery, whereupon shortly after training he was to find himself posted to North Africa. As a forward observation officer (responsible for calling in artillery, fire and 'fall of shot' corrections) in late October 1942, he accompanied a group of commandos around the El Alamein area, whose mission was raiding behind German lines by means of night infiltration, destroying Axis fuel dumps and weakening German mobility.

After one such raid, a navigation error saw them captured by the Germans, whose strict stance concerning British commandos was that they were to be shot. Receiving 'rough treatment' things were looking bleak, then chance intervened when a German 'senior officer' wished to inspect the 'Commando prisoners'. It was none other than the Desert Fox, Rommel himself, to whom Sean O'Donovan spoke up, telling Rommel of the treatment they had received and that they were going to be shot. Impressed by his impertinence and his cheeky forwardness, Rommel rewarded his brazen boldness by granting the group a reprieve from death. They were imprisoned in Tobruk, North Africa, but within two weeks he and two colleagues affected an escape, only to subsequently fall foul of the immensity of the desert and were recaptured. This time they were handed over to the Italian Army, transferred to Reggio in Italy via Palermo in Sicily, whereupon Sean once again escaped and joined the Italian partisans (resistance) in Calabria, alongside whom he fought for a hugely exciting nine months.

Informed upon, he was once again captured and faced death a second time. Using a certain amount of Irish 'blarney' he manged to convince the English-speaking prison camp chaplain, who had learned his English from Irish priests in Rome, to persuade the Italian Camp Commandant to give him a reprieve. This he was granted but he was again transferred, this time to Luckenwalde POW Camp in Germany. For some reason, the Germans placed all the 'Irish by birth, Irish by extraction, Irish by choice and Irish by chance' in one POW camp. Using, among others, the classification of one's surname by 'O', a mixed grouping resulted in the group including some from America and even one from Sierra Leone on the west coast of Africa. With a number of escape attempts foiled at their early stages, it dawned on the inmates that there must be a German 'plant' or plants among them, so those that could resorted to speaking Irish to each other. The Germans responded with a 'get tough' regime: food restrictions, Red Cross food parcels failed to appear and conditions generally deteriorated within the camp. Orders were issued that letters to next-of-kin allowed under the Geneva Convention would not pass the camp's censor unless they were written in English.

It was about this time that a letter arrived in Dublin, written in English and describing conditions in Luckenwalde POW camp as being, to say the least, quite acceptable. The letter ended quite innocently with the words, 'Give my love to Moryha.' Since no such lady existed, it was not too difficult to translate 'Moryha' into the Gaelic words '*mar dheadh*' and from this it became apparent that the letter contained a deliberate tissue of lies. As a result of this, immediate representations were made to the International Red Cross in Geneva and in due course a delegation from Switzerland arrived in Luckenwalde to investigate. Naturally, by the time they arrived, conditions had improved beyond belief, and all as a result of a simple Irish word.

Sean O'Donovan escaped from Luckenwalde not long afterwards but was soon recaptured. In order to teach him a lesson he was stripped of his clothing, put in a goods wagon and sent by train to Neuruppin work camp near Berlin. The German capital in April 1945 was being regularly bombed by the RAF by night and the USAF by day and Sean, along with the other inmates, were organised into work parties to clear the resultant rubble, debris, fragments of stone, brick and other masonry off the roads. They were not allowed to enter the air raid shelters during bombing raids so it was very dangerous work. Being marched along a road one day, the route was choked with retreating German Army and fleeing refugees. Suddenly, two Russian fighter aircraft strafed the scene. Seizing a German military map from an overturned vehicle and noticing it was of the local area, on the spur of the moment Sean seized on the opportunity provided by the confusion and pandemonium going on around him, and decided to make a break for it, and he walked away unnoticed.

A number of days later, in a shell-shattered copse of woods northwest of Berlin, he was noticed by a band of men, a group of twenty Russian Cossacks on horseback. Not on sleek, slender cavalry mounts, rather these were unspectacular short and shaggy animals, more like ponies, their riders brandishing Thompson machine guns. Their leader, also armed with a sword, was ex-Navy and as a seaman in a previous existence had been to Dublin. Together, the Cossack leader, Thomas, and Prisoner Number 142345 (Sean O'Donovan, shortened to '345') sang the First World War favourite, 'It's a long way to Tipperary'. Sean was given a pony with a bloodstained saddle and thereafter rode with the Cossacks. It was on horseback that he entered Berlin, having shared with the Cossacks their vodka and rations. Handed over to the Allies, three years of undernourishment saw him sent to hospital in England.

Repatriated and recuperated, Sean O'Donovan stayed in the British Army after the war, retiring after a full, long and distinguished career in the rank of regimental sergeant-major. His brother, Fred O'Donovan, having been bitten by the 'entertainment bug' when involved with amateur theatricals to relieve the tedium while convalescing with TB, entered show business, becoming a director/producer in the Gaiety Theatre, Jury's Irish Cabaret, head of Eamonn Andrews Studios, Chairman of the RTÉ Authority and the National Concert Hall. Sean and Fred O'Donovan survived the war and went on to live very full and purposeful lives.

Back on Juno Beach, there were Irishmen who did not survive the day. On 16 June 1944, Lucy Stewart in Vancouver, Canada, received the following:

MINISTER OF NATIONAL DEFENCE DEEPLY REGRETS TO INFORM YOU THAT K29061 LANCE SERGEANT WILLIAM FRANCIS STEWART HAS BEEN OFFICIALLY REPORTED WOUNDED IN ACTION SIXTH JUNE 1944 AND DIED OF WOUNDS SEVENTH JUNE 1944 STOP IF ANY FURTHER INFORMATION BECOMES AVAILABLE IT WILL BE FORWARDED AS SOON AS RECEIVED

DIRECTOR OF RECORDS

Among those who waded ashore in the first wave of Canadian troops on Juno was 42-year-old Sergeant William Francis Stewart from Ramelton, County Donegal. He was the eldest son of Sir Henry Stewart, a baronet whose financial difficulties forced many of the family to emigrate, and so it was that during the 1920s William went to Canada in the hope of finding a new life. William married and took a job as a longshoreman. On 6 June 1944 his mother, Lady Mary, still made her home in Letterkenny, County Donegal. Back on Juno her son led a six-man engineer team, part of 2 Platoon, 6th Field Company, Royal Canadian Engineers, in support of the Royal Winnipeg Rifles. Arriving near Courseulles, they had a torrid time and battled through heavy mortar and machine-gun fire, sustaining heavy casualties as they advanced. William survived through this difficulty, however late in the day he fell victim to a German sniper and was severely wounded, dying the next day.

One year later, his wife Lucy received notification of what would be coming home of her husband's personal possessions. The list was as follows:

1 Fountain Pen 'Everybodys'.
1 Evershop Pencil 'Sheaffers'.

1 Gold Wedding Ring.

1 Leather Wallet.

1 Cigarette Lighter.

Photographs.

'Canada, World War II Service Files of War Dead' documents nearly 45,000 Canadians who lost their lives. Among them, 136 of these files relate to Irish-born men who lost their lives in Canadian service. Others to die in Normandy were Martin Crawford (34) from Ballycastle, County Antrim; Harry Cummings (22) from Portrush, County Antrim; Ralph Tupper Ferns (24), from Cahir, County Tipperary; Arthur Price (37) from Drumshanbo, County Leitrim (a lumberjack and ex-member of the Irish Guards); and Michael Rogan (20), a Canadian Irishman whose parents were from Dromara, County Down. Arthur Price and Michael Rogan were involved in the struggle for the possession of the Abbaye d'Ardenne, located just beyond the northern outskirts of Caen. Its ultimate possession proved hard fought for and hard gained, but eventually they drove the 12th SS Hitler-Jugend from the abbey. There they discovered the remains of a number of Canadian servicemen who had been summarily executed by the SS after their capture immediately following D-Day, actions for which SS Commander Kurt Meyer was tried and sentenced to life imprisonment following the war.

Inaccurate aerial and naval bombardment had left the defences on Omaha, Gold and now Juno virtually intact. German coastal and shore batteries, observation, anti-tank and machine-gun bunkers went largely undamaged. Naval bombardment proved more effective than aerial bomber bombardment, with typhoon fighter bombers proving greater accuracy still, though not achieving the desired effect overall. With the deployment of the DD tanks delayed due to rough seas, disembarkation from the landing craft had to be made under direct fire, and in consequence heavy casualties were sustained by B Company, Royal Winnipeg Rifles while landing. Relatively unscathed by the bombing, the strong points and machine-gun emplacements had to be cleared by the grim prospect of direct assault. Further west along the beach, D Company faced less defensive fire as it was beyond the range of the strong points, though the beach was not totally undefended. The King's (Liverpool) Regiment, 8th Irish Battalion, formed the 7th Beach Group on Juno on 6 June.

The King's (Liverpool) Regiment had transhipped from the HMS *Ulster Monarch*, formerly a passenger ship on the Liverpool–Belfast route, down scramble nets, jumping into the pitching landing craft on the order, 'jump now!' and made their way to shore. On board the landing craft 'the tension was terrific', according to Jim Fitzsimons in his book, *The Liverpool 8th Irish Battalion at War 1939–45*. Wading ashore, initially in chest-high water with his rifle held above his head and enemy fire bursting all around them, Fitzsimons and the Kings Regiment fought their way inland near Graye-sur-Mer to contribute in quelling the German resistance. Major Max Morrison, A Company, was first man ashore on Juno Beach and led a bayonet charge on a German machine-gun post. The successful charge led to him being awarded the Military Cross. Proceeding up the beach, they established a command post on the sand dunes. B Company under Major O'Brien was not so fortunate. They suffered from the late arrival of the 'advance' party and DD tanks and both he, his second in command and others were wounded, exposed as they were to machine-gun fire.

Frank McLoughlin from Dublin, a wireless operator serving with the RAF and Combined Operations Special Forces, landed with the 3rd Canadian Division on Juno, as did fellow Dubliner William Joseph Clarke, also RAF. He was an armourer's assistant, part of 3205 Servicing Commando. These were small groups of engineers who were tasked with setting up operations, under fire if necessary, including fuel, spare parts and ammunition. They would carry all of their tools and equipment with them through an assault landing, and were well able to defend themselves.

J.S. (Josh) Honan from County Clare was a cadet in Class No. 7 in the Military College, Irish Defence Forces in 1933. He subsequently joined the British Army and was involved in the D-Day landings as part of a 'mixed' engineer and infantry pre-assault party on a sector of Juno Beach with the Canadian 3rd Division. Writing in the January 1982 edition of *An Cosantóir*, the Irish Defence Forces journal, he tells us that he was 'volunteered' by his commanding officer and attached to the 5th Canadian Assault Engineers.

They were to land at ten minutes before H-Hour (H-Hour-10) to dismantle as many mines as possible and to try and 'bounce' some of the other beach obstacles out of the way, all in an effort to make gaps for the DD swimming tanks and AVREs which would precede the first wave of assault.

However, everything did not go quite as planned; their landing craft went aground with its closed ramp jammed against a mined obstacle. Josh Honan went over the side, and together with his 'sapper' partner, disarmed the mine and shouted for those in front of the landing craft to get over the side and help push it back until it floated and the ramp could be lowered. As soon as the ramp came down, the Canadian infantry were out and off up the beach like hares, straight into a 'hot' sector. Many were cut down by exploding shells, mortar and machine-gun fire. Meanwhile, Josh Honan was sitting astride steel girders, with his legs locked underneath for purchase, and with stiff fingers from immersion in the cold sea continued his sensitive work of dealing with trip wires and detonators.

The tide had now risen, and each wave covered his head. Buoyancy was also an issue, the current pulling him this way and that, creating its own hazards. Landing craft were now arriving thick and fast, being literally hurled onto the beach by the wind and waves, and the danger of being blown up or run down had increased dramatically with each new wave of explosions that were being set off. It was now wiser and safer to go ashore, so he launched himself towards the sea wall where he was helped over by willing hands.

The King's (Liverpool) Regiment, 8th Irish Battalion's task as the 7th Beach Group was to secure positions on the beach, provide defence against counter-attack, maintain organisation by directing troops and vehicles inland, locate and mark minefields and collect the wounded and the dead. All this they achieved, to a greater and lesser degree, while initially under fire until immediate German resistance was subdued. They continued to take sporadic artillery fire and intermittent mortar fire, and even the following day, 7 June, a lone Luftwaffe fighter bombed the beach with a single shell, killing fifteen and wounding seven, a sight 'which was appalling to see,' according to Jim Fitzsimons. 'Our signal officer was wounded in a Bren gun carrier vehicle and our sergeant was delayed in reaching us. Instead a "Deputy" sergeant, J.J. Murphy (22), had to take over as signal officer and sergeant.' The 8th Irish

Battalion remained on Juno Beach for six weeks in their capacity as Beach Group Unit.

Also arriving on D-Day was the Very Reverend Cyril Patrick Crean, the youngest of four sons of a Dublin barrister, who were all educated at Belvedere College, Dublin. His uncle, Major Thomas Joseph Crean, VC, DSO, another Belvederean, was a surgeon who won the Victoria Cross in the Boer War and the DSO in the First World War. 'Father Paddy' had served as a curate in several Dublin parishes prior to his becoming a British Army Roman Catholic Chaplain in 1941. He landed on D-Day at Juno Beach at Bernières-sur-Mer with the 29th Armoured Brigade. He was awarded an MBE on 24 January 1946 for his wartime service; his citation read as follows:

Father Crean has been the Roman Catholic Senior Chaplain within 1 Corps throughout the campaign in North West Europe. Possessing a quiet, sincere and likeable character, he has always been on the best of terms with all ranks. He has never spared himself in his work and has afforded great assistance and comfort to many.

He has made constant visits to the wounded, often in advanced medical posts and has, throughout, shown great keenness and organising ability in arranging clubs and rest rooms which have not been confined to those of his own creed. During the early days of the bridgehead he did invaluable work in locating the burial places and identifying the bodies of unknown airmen who had crashed and had been reported missing. This work, voluntarily undertaken by him, must have been of inestimable comfort to the airmen's next of kin.

He has been a strong rock to those of his own flock, and has throughout taken the greatest interest in all matters pertaining to the welfare of the troops. He has set a very fine example and has made a great contribution to the happiness and wellbeing of the men.

In 1955, the Very Reverend Crean was appointed head chaplain of the Irish Defence Forces because of his wartime experiences, and in 1960 and 1962 he accompanied battalions of the Irish Defence Forces to the Congo as part of the United Nations Peacekeeping Force. In September 1962, he retired from the Irish Defence Forces and was appointed parish priest of

Donnybrook, Dublin. He died on 10 August 1973, having two months previously celebrated the fortieth anniversary of his ordination.

Another person 'of the cloth' but already in situ was Kathleen (Kitty) Walsh from Blarney, County Cork. 'Sister Fabian' was assigned to a convent in the market town of Eu in Normandy in September 1939, having been sent to Paris in mid July 1939 to complete her Novitiate in the Maison Mère. She was to stay in the country for fifteen years, witnessing the horrors that the Second World War would bring. In the course of the war she was to move to the Saint-Calais Convent in Laval, which was among the first convents to be bombed by the Nazis and later by the Allies. Liberated after D-Day, it was the Canadian Division that eventually reached them first: 'Their triumphal entry would have to be seen, words would not describe it. The return of an All-Ireland winning team would be in the shade compared to it.' Over the days other Allied forces followed, with the people cheering the columns of troops as they went past, throwing them bottles of champagne. This was in stark contrast to her memory of three days after she had moved into the convent, when:

> The German army in massive strength poured into the town and occupied it. Endless rows of young lads in their teens marching by, so well-groomed in their green military uniforms. They were strictly disciplined, having been trained from a young age in the Fuhrer's Youth Camps. The pity of it all; idealistic youth being so misguided by a fanatical thirst for power.

Sister Fabian returned to Cork in June 1952 after fifteen years in France and died on 15 May 2007.

It was to stop this 'fanatical thirst for power', so aptly described by Sister Fabian that the Allies, Irishmen among them, invaded France to drive through Belgium, the Netherlands and into Germany itself, fighting for the restoration of freedom, the liberation of Europe and to make the world safe again.

II
SWORD BEACH

The landing areas of Sword Beach, which ran west from Ouistreham at the mouth of the River Orne to Lion-sur-Mer, were mostly featureless, devoid of any obvious reference points. The coastline along Sword, the fifth and final of the invasion beaches, was remarkable by being unremarkable. There was scarcely a singular striking feature to any of the sites along it, nothing particularly noticeable or noteworthy in terms of readily apparent identification points on its low-lying length that easily differentiated one place from another. Required to deliver troops to a specific point on the beach, this uncommon topographical banality was a problem for the Royal Navy.

One hour before dawn on D-Day, the solution discretely rose from the sea bed. Two Royal Navy midget submarines, X-20 and X-23, broke cover at 0430 hours a quarter of a mile offshore. Each slowly extended a telescopic mast to a height of eighteen feet to act as a navigational aid for the first wave of British landing craft as they approached the beach. Aware they could be vulnerable to 'friendly fire', a large ensign was flown to clearly indicate they were Royal Navy.

Intelligence assessments, reconnaissance reports and operational estimates of enemy strengths and weaknesses meant the beaches selected for the invasion were not arbitrary sweeps of sand chosen by chance, but instead were carefully considered. The planners had weighed the risks against the requirements, and as accuracy of execution was called for it was the mission of the two 50-foot 'X-Craft' midget submarines to make that happen.

This top-secret task, codenamed Operation Gambit, ensured the need for navigational precision was met. Towed across the English Channel on the night of 2 June, they took up their respective positions and submerged, ready for the time to emerge from the sea bed, appear on the surface and act like beacons to guide the landing craft to their objectives.

In the event, due to the delayed H-Hour and the postponement of D-Day itself by twenty-four hours from 5 June to 6 June due to bad weather, the two small submarines had to remain submerged for sixty hours in total. The two five-man crews had to withstand the pressure of being confined in cramped conditions and remain undetected, maintaining radio silence until it was operationally time to reveal themselves and ensure the Sword landings were free from navigational error. Their mission cleverly and creatively accomplished, it was now up to those on the landing craft to carry out their tasks, chiefly to clear the beach defences of enemy, connect with the British paratroopers at Pegasus Bridge and capture Caen, seven miles inland.

The invasion of Normandy on 6 June 1944 was an onslaught, and the enormous beach, coastal and inland fortifications prepared in depth under Field Marshal Edwin Rommel could only be overcome by overwhelming force. The ability of the Allies to marshal this military might undetected had taken the Germans completely by surprise. The British landings on Sword Beach went smoother than the Allies experienced on Juno. The aerial bombardment and withering naval salvos onto German shore strong points curtailed the damage the defenders could inflict on the assault but, as ever, with manned defences and obstacles in place, it was not without its difficulties. Losses were inflicted from indirect inland artillery fire hitting landing craft and causing casualties on the beach, and the pouring of heavy small-arms fire by a determined German defence from their strong point at La Broche took three hours to overcome. However, on Sword the specialised assault armour carried out the functions they were created for to good effect.

The successive waves of landing craft followed a schedule and plan prepared to achieve the capabilities they were designed for and the outcomes desired of them. DD tanks, AVREs, and two separate waves of two infantry companies each; a Beach Group, Bulldozers and more AVREs, self-propelled guns, a full squadron of tanks, artillery guns and finally stores and ammunition, was how each Brigade was timetabled to be brought ashore, beginning with the first wave at H-Hour minus five minutes, the last at H-Hour plus 120 minutes. The schedule was not maintained, as per plan, after H-Hour plus thirty minutes or so but it did see the first five or six waves arrive as planned before confused intermixing occurred. It was a good start by the British 3rd Infantry Division.

At its forefront, clanking down the landing craft ramp at 0710 hours with six AVREs, specially designed for beach obstacle breaching and clearing operations, Captain Redmond Cunningham from Waterford, 1st Troop Leader, 5 Assault Regiment, 79th Assault Squadron of the Royal Engineers moved along the beach. Papers donated in 1994 by Redmond Cunningham himself to the Manuscript and Archive Research Library of Trinity College Dublin, tell the story in his own words. He was to become one of the most highly decorated Irish officers serving in the British Army during the Second World War, and he received the Military Cross for his actions on D-Day.

Five minutes before, the specialised armour of the 79th Assault Squadron of the Royal Engineers deployed their 'tanks that could swim'. These were vulnerable to being swamped by waves in the choppy water, which was what happened at Omaha, but on Sword thirty-one DD tanks and AVREs were successfully deployed. The canvas sides of these Duplex Drive tanks protruded a foot above water level and wrapped completely around it. This canvas wraparound contained tubes that when inflated with compressed air allowed the tank to float. What gave it motion, allowing it 'to swim' was that the Sherman tank's engine was connected to two propellers. Sometimes likened to 'floating canvas bath tubs', they could reach a speed of four knots. A weapon of surprise, they gave very welcome close-in support to the landing British infantry, while at the same time causing shock to the German defenders, but none were in evidence on the section of the beach on which Captain Redmond Cunningham's No. 1 Troop, 5 Assault Regiment landed.

Their LCT had been loaded with six AVREs in the order of disembarkation that the exigencies of breaching and overcoming the beach obstacles to be encountered demanded. First off, two mine-clearing flails of the 'Crab' tank, then the troop commander's tank, followed by the 'Bridge' tank and the 'Fascine', with its bundle of logs designed to fill in anti-tank ditches. Bringing up the rear was the 'Bobbin', with its metal 'carpet' to make the path across soft going terrain (mud or quicksand) accessible. The other varieties of modified tanks, the 'Crocodiles' – flame-throwing tanks with a range of 150 yards – the 'Petard' tanks with their bunker-busting spigot mortar heavy gun, and 'Firefly' tanks (Shermans with the British 17-pounder anti-tank gun mounted on them) would follow, like the armoured bulldozers, not far behind subsequent assault waves.

Everything on board LCT went according to plan; air photographs helping to identify beach landmarks. When approximately 1 mile off, the OC and I spotted what we thought to be landmarks for No.1 Troop Lane. Observation became more difficult as we approached the beach owing to smoke etc. caused by the bombardment. When we were about 500 yards offshore the smoke cleared and I observed our craft was approximately opposite the point where I wanted to touch down, so I told this to the [Landing] Craft Commander and mounted my AVRE. As the craft came into the beach it veered to the starboard and touched down approximately 200 yards to the right of where I had hoped it would.

The troop then disembarked in order. IG, IH ['Crabs with mine clearing flails], IA [Troop Leader], OA [OCs AVRE], IB [Bridge] and IC [Bobbin]. This disembarkation took place in between 3 and 4 feet of water.

IG [Crab with flail] proceeded up the beach and started flailing just about water level [this Armoured Vehicle Assault Engineer Tank was a Sherman fitted with a revolving drum on the front to which heavy chains were attached. The drum was fixed to the tank by two girders. The drums revolved causing the chains to strike the ground, setting off any mines buried under the surface]. I called him up and he said he suspected mines. Shortly after this there was an explosion and he stopped. By this time all the AVREs were off the craft and backing into the sea and I was searching the beach for enemy opposition. IG being useless, I ordered IH [the other 'crab' with flails] forward and followed in his tracks, instructing IG to cover our left where the enemy appeared to be firing [from]. Under my directions IH now flailed up to the dunes whilst I remained below HWM [high water mark] and with IG engaged a Pill Box target on the left. My AVRE was twice hit low down. When the lane was ready I ordered IB to drop his bridge. He did so and it appeared to fall low, but he could not improve it as I ordered because it had been struck by a shell. The commander [Stephen Young] and some of his crew dismounted and freed the AVRE from the bridge, thus enabling IH ['Crab' with flail] followed by IA to cross over the bridge. With the help of Sergeant Young's party IC [Bobbin] jettisoned his Bangalore and drove over the bridge dropping his log carpet at the top.

In this manner the gap was made good. IH was flailing down the exit when he was blown up by a mine, so I ordered Sergeant Young to obtain mine detectors and proceed with clearance, while I contacted the squadron by W/T wireless telephone and asked for another flail. While proceeding down the beach on foot I found a flail [Crab tank] sitting in the water doing nothing, so I brought him up. He proceeded down the exit on the left of IH and I followed in his tracks in IA. As I passed [it] IA, I encountered a mine and the tank was blown up. Two of my crew who were marking the gap received shock through blast. I dismounted and after a very quick reconnaissance decided to make a new exit along [the] beach lateral and an exit on the right of the one I had been working on, so with my own [mine] detector, one a sergeant from Division Royal Engineers possessed and an auxiliary row of prodders, we proceeded with clearance. The mines uncovered were French anti-tank and appeared to have been laid a long time. I inspected for booby traps but found none. The mines were thickly sewn, approximately one per half yard of front or closer.

Whilst this was proceeding I sent Sergeant Botcherley to see if Sergeant Nye could be found as he had a plough [and was engaged in beach clearance]. Sergeant Botcherley returned and said he could not find Sergeant Nye.

The lane was declared clear at 9.05 hours, but as scattered mines were still being found I kept a prodding party working on the verges.

Then with the help of a bulldozer a second gap was made alongside the bridge and IC was called upon to jettison the B Bangalore and drop the carpet in this new gap. This was successful and I remained at this exit, blowing telegraph poles, demolishing corners of dangerous houses etc. until approximately 1300 hours then with the remains of 2 Troop and Sergeant Sawyer which I had collected, I went to Squadron Rally.

I visited the CCS [Casualty Collection Station] beaches in search of Sergeant Nye or crew but found no trace of them although his tank was burning on the beach.

From about 0815 hours to 1200 hours the lane we were working on was under very heavy mortar fire and both Sergeants Young and Tittny displayed qualities of courage and coolness in handling their men.

The Troop as a whole were calm and acted promptly to my orders, in several cases displaying initiative.

The flails, whilst not useful owing to the nature of the ground, were very hard working and from Lieutenant Boal's 75, probably saved IA from destruction.

Sergeant Manning deserves mention for the efficient manner in which he carried out his job, his continual perseverance and courage overcoming all obstacles.

R.C. Cunningham
Captain RE
12 June 1944

Captain Cunningham's No. 1 Troop Leader's summary of breaching operations for his sector of Sword Beach gives an authentic account of the effort involved and the struggle to successfully clear lanes through the obstacles on the beach, so that the waves of tanks and infantry arriving later could proceed unhindered through the exits off the beach. It is interesting to note his remark about being under very heavy mortar fire almost throughout (0815 hours to 1200 hours) because the lethal effect of being mortared is well illustrated by the experience of Private James Murray from Dublin, 2nd King's Own Shropshire Light Infantry. A mortar round landed between him and a comrade, the mortar's blast blowing his companion apart. One moment the two men were together, the next, shockingly, he was no longer there. All that was found was a fragment of his rifle and a portion of his boot. Private Murray inexplicably remained physically unharmed.

Such horrors can haunt someone for the rest of their lives, as also can those inflicted by one's own side. The gruesomely hideous use of flamethrowers against German pillboxes, the screams of the young German soldiers inside, some still boys, as they literally burned alive, and the sight afterwards of the bodies reduced to blackened bare bone. All flesh was incinerated, seared to ashes, and all that remained were charred skeletons where once was precious life, loved ones and hope. These images psychologically impacted on an individual, and were not easily lived with. Marking the psyche, the awfulness never fully left them.

The second wave, the 2nd Battalion Royal Ulster Rifles, landed on Sword, their way cleared of beach obstacles by an Irishman from Waterford and his troop. They proceeded up the beach through the lanes breached by the assault engineers gone before them to find the fortified concrete pillbox beach defences intact and the defenders inside them still active. Rifleman John Shanahan from Cork was among 'the Rifles':

> We hit Sword Beach just after 0900 hrs. Actually, we landed in about 4 feet of water. I remember my big concern was not to get my rifle wet. The landing area was heavily defended and we met mortar and heavy gun fire. Of course there were some soldiers who did not manage to get as far as the beach. Once ashore, our battleships continued their heavy bombardment inland. Although we met strong resistance, we had to be careful not to advance too fast and overtake their reach. The enemy were in strength but they retreated to the fall-back position in the woods inland of the beach area.

Jack Allshire, from Crosshaven, County Cork, was a member of D Company 2nd Battalion Royal Ulster Rifles, a Company commanded by Captain John

Richard St Leger Aldworth, also from County Cork (Newmarket). Their Battalion was part of the 9th Infantry Brigade of the 3rd British Division. When the ship which brought them across the English Channel arrived off Sword Beach, the German defences were being pounded by the Royal Navy battleships and he watched in awe as shell after shell exploded on enemy positions. However, some German artillery units remained intact and as the Battalion prepared to go ashore shells continued to fall into the sea around them. One shell actually smashed into the stern of Jack Allshire's ship but it failed to explode. Noticing that the first among them had a difficult time getting ashore, because they were weighed down with their backpacks and bicycles – and some almost drowned – Jack and other members of the unit hurled their bicycles over the side and waded ashore without them.

As the men stumbled onto the beach, mortar bombs and artillery shells continued to explode in their vicinity. When he moved forward, Jack caught his first sight of the enemy when he spotted some German prisoners being marched to a holding area with their hands raised above their heads, but he would soon have a close encounter of a more dangerous kind. After they left the beach, the 2nd Battalion Royal Ulster Rifles under Lieutenant Colonel Ian Harris from Tipperary made their way half a mile inland to the small village of Lion-sur-Mer, which had been designated as the Battalion assembly point. From there they moved to the high ground near the village of Périers-sur-le-Dan, where they dug in for the night. Throughout the day, transport troop carrier planes flew overhead ferrying reinforcements inland, among them the 1st Battalion Royal Ulster Rifles, those Allied glider-borne invaders who had gone in pre-H-Hour with the 6th Airborne Division.

Connecting up with the 7th Parachute Regiment, which had secured the previously gained Pegasus Bridge by the glider-borne 'Ox and Bucks' (of whom 10 per cent were Irish), was the task of No. 6 Commando 1st Special Service Brigade. Among them was Galwegian Private Patrick 'Paddy' Gillen, who had previously served with the 4th Royal Norfolk Regiment. Trained in Inverness-shire at the Commando Training Centre, the instruction regime there was necessarily arduous as these specialist troops were to be relied upon to perform in particularly difficult and tiring circumstances. 'Battle Fitness' was paramount, and they had to develop a toughness, tenacity and teamwork beyond that of regular troops. They faced many miles of forced route marches and cross country runs with complete kit, needed to be confident and competent in skills like abseiling and water work, and overall required a high degree of endurance. Night work and marksmanship was required to be achieved before the much coveted Commando Green Beret could be successfully laid claim to. Thereafter, their training became 'mission specific' to the tasks they were to undertake on D-Day. Landing in twenty-two landing craft, four were hit directly by shell fire before they reached the beach while others were damaged:

> The order was given to lower ramps [near the far eastern end of the beach by La Brèche] and we began to pour out of the landing craft in single file, with weapons kept above our heads to keep them dry. We were moving as fast as our pack-laden bodies would carry us and I saw many bodies floating in the sea and lying on the beach. We didn't find out until later that night who was dead, wounded or missing from our unit. Some tanks were hit but it was a welcome sight to see how many got ashore and it lifted our morale no end.

Even elite troops appreciated close in support on D-Day. Moving off the beach as rapidly as they could, the Commandos pursued a rapid and vigorous fighting advance inland, conducting assaults against enemy pillboxes and strong points as they progressed. Snipers were a torment to them: 'The whole thing was to move fast. Not to be an object for the snipers because if they picked you out you were likely to soon be dead or wounded. We had good officers and they insisted on us maintaining [a] rapid momentum over the 6 mile advance.'

Reaching and linking up with the Airborne was the task at hand, and shortly after 1 pm the Allied ground troops arrived to the bridges (Pegasus and Horsa), linked up with the troops holding them and reinforced and supported the 7th Paratroopers, securing the area beyond. To do so they had first to cross the bridges, and although in British hands, German snipers were still active in the vicinity. That evening they moved to high ground on Saulnier Farm near Amfreville and dug in.

'Digging in' is what ground troops do to occupy and hold an area, usually on high ground known as 'key terrain', the seizure and maintaining of which bestows a marked advantage on whoever has possession. As the name implies, trenches are dug, firing positions excavated and overhead protection built, all of which is camouflaged and strict occupation discipline imposed. Depth is added to the defensive position by the siting of trenches over distance rearwards, to prevent the 'objective' being easily overrun. Support weapon trenches are sited tactically throughout, bearing in mind the mission and nature of the terrain. Well dug in troops can be difficult to dislodge. This done, Paddy Gillen and his comrades in 6th Commando opened their backpacks and cooked up a well-deserved hot meal, their vital mission of helping to secure the eastern flank of the Bridgehead ahead of them. That night they received harassing fire from German artillery and casualties were suffered. Unknown to them, the Germans were only 500 yards away.

Back on Sword Beach, around midday Captain Redmond Cunningham, 79th Assault Squadron, had been ordered with ten AVREs to advance on, seize and hold the bridge and lock gates at Ouistreham. Catching the Germans on the near side of the lock gates by surprise, these were mostly immediately overcome. Far stiffer resistance was received by those Germans on the far side though, they even managed to partially destroy one side of the bridge. Using the not inconsiderable firepower of the ten AVREs, in the subsequent intense exchange the bridge and lock gates were wrestled from the Germans. These were successfully held overnight, a duration which saw 'active' patrolling under Captain Cunningham's direction and resulting in the capture of enemy positions and materials and German soldiers being killed and taken prisoner. Captain Redmond Cunningham continued to fight throughout the rest of the war, earning a bar to the Military Cross awarded for his actions on D-Day. At war's end he qualified as an architect, and set up and became involved in many successful business ventures in Waterford. He died in 1999.

Informed that he was too young and skinny to join the Irish Army, Sean Deegan from Dublin crossed the border at the age of seventeen and seeking adventure joined the RAF 405 Repair and Salvage Unit (R&SU). Now nineteen, on D-Day he landed at Sword Beach. He was given a Harley Davidson motorbike and tasked with reconnaissance missions to locate and salvage crashed Allied aircraft. Nearly shot from his Harley Davidson by US troops on one occassion, an American major gave him his battledress and he became 'an honorary US major'. Sean Deegan was to find the exciting exploits he sought, his experiences bringing him to an understanding of the true horror of war and particularly the Nazi regime. He was to survive the war and by the time he returned to Ireland he was a convinced and committed pacifist. He joined the Franciscan Order and became Brother Columbanus.

Landing on Sword also was Lieutenant Peter Wilson, 45 Commando, believed to be one of the first 'killed in action'. County Clare native John Egan (24), from Milltown Malbay, of 41 Royal Marine Commando also landed on Sword Beach. Although he made it off the beach on D-Day, the next day he was KIA and is buried at Hermanville War Cemetery at Hermanville-sur-Mer.

Directed by the Luftwaffe 2nd Fighter Corps HQ, at 0900 on D-Day morning, two German Messerschmitt Bf 109 fighter aircraft took off from an airfield near Lille. The pilots had first to organise their ground crews to move to Poix, where all German fighter squadrons were being consolidated. They came in very low from the east and strafed along the sands of Sword Beach, and in an instant they were blazing away on Juno and moving quickly onto Omaha. Manoeuvring through barrage balloons, they were up into the clouds and gone. This morning raid by the two solitary FW 109s appears to be the only recorded enemy fighter attack along the invasion beaches. Daring also was an audacious raid by three German E-boats, who managed to let loose nearly twenty torpedoes and sink the Norwegian destroyer HNoMS *Svenner*, killing over thirty crew members. Having broken in two, her bow and stern sticking up to form a perfect 'V', the *Svenner* slipped beneath the waves off Sword Beach.

The German 21st Panzer Division, which had been training and refitting south of Caen, also attacked the Allied troops as they landed on the Normandy coast. Their counter-attack had been hampered by confusion, delayed orders and the Allied bombing of Caen, causing damage and destruction to the region that took time to circumvent. The time afforded was well used by

Allies to place anti-tank guns on high ground on the likely approach of the German tanks. On the Panzers arrival, the British were ready and executed fire to good effect. Notwithstanding, a number of tanks broke through to the coast, but with insufficient numbers and no infantry support they could not capitalise on their limited success. By not advancing on Caen, and in fact not taking advantage of their own overall success when perhaps it was open for them to do so, the 3rd British Division's third – perhaps overambitious – objective went unachieved. It was also a day that saw Tipperary man Lieutenant Colonel Ian Harris, Officer Commanding 2nd Battalion Royal Ulster Rifles, take temporary command of the British 9th Brigade on the wounding and evacuation of Brigadier J.C. Cunningham MC.

In February 2016, more than seventy years after the D-Day landings, twenty-one veterans from Northern Ireland were awarded France's highest honour, the Legion d'Honneur. The awards were personally presented by President Francois Hollande during a ceremony at Thiepval Barracks in Lisburn, County Antrim. George Thompson served as a telegraphist in the Royal Navy. On D-Day he was part of a commando unit and landed on Sword Beach, acting as a radio link between naval and shore ships, calling in gunfire onto enemy positions. They were among the first to land on D-Day, and guided in the assault group. Of the 129 Commandos in his unit there were only four left after Normandy. He landed on the beach when he was seventeen and was there for his eighteenth birthday. Interviewed by the media on the occasion, he stated, 'We were well trained for it; we were trained all the time. It was just like an exercise in its own way; only the ones who went down didn't get up again.' Asked about the long-term effects of exposure to wartime experiences, he answered:

> Somebody once asked me did I ever dream after the war. A psychiatrist once told us, talk about it. She was right. When you start talking about it, you forget about it. When you are keeping it inside, you have nightmares. When you talk about it, it seems to leave. I don't look back; I just live my life, believe it or not, and drink dark rum.

Ireland was regarded as having been largely untouched by the war but some of the 'D-Day Irish' were touched in ways that people neither understood nor acknowledged at the time, or since. Maybe this was true of themselves too, many remaining at war within. The Franciscan, Brother Columbanus, formerly the 'too young and too skinny' John Deegan, who found himself arriving on Sword Beach with a Harley Davidson motorbike at nineteen and subsequently riding through France into Belgium and Holland, was involved in the 'Battle of the Bulge' (Ardennes) and the invasion of Germany: 'When we went to Germany, we found out it was a worthwhile cause.' He had heard stories of German concentration camps but only came to understand the true horror of the Nazi regime when he witnessed the Belsen death camp for himself. 'That was it for me; I knew there was no glamour in war.' The war had brought him from adventurer through pacifist to priest. With the Franciscan order he spent time in Drogheda, Rome and twenty-five years in County Waterford, but he could never forget the horror of what he witnessed at Belsen: 'I couldn't shake off the smell of death I experienced that day. I sometimes get flashbacks and the smell returns as if it was yesterday.'

For Private James Murray from Dublin, 2nd King's Own Shropshire Light Infantry, it was the 'sound' of the screams of the young German soldiers in the pillboxes as they burned alive inside following the use of flamethrowers, while for Michael d'Alton, Royal Navy, it was the sight of the quiet and smooth descent to death of the tank crew exiting the landing craft, and the random death of the little boy on the beach, 'blown up' playing football, that stayed with him. The thoughts, sights, sounds and smell of war were horrific, and for many they were the enemy within themselves thereafter. But the greater horror had been stopped, and like John Deegan (Brother Columbanus) they knew that 'it was a worthwhile cause'.

12

D-DAY PLUS

Getting the right items to the right place at the right time in the right quantities helps to make the plan happen. Organising and designing a force of specific size and ensuring its composition meets the unique task or mission to be undertaken also assists the effort. Planning, supporting, commanding and fighting D-Day was an enormous undertaking, and it was very well executed. By nightfall on D-Day the Allies had breached Hitler's Atlantic Wall, and the hopes of opening a second front were now more than an aspiration. A foothold had been secured and having this lodgement allowed them to bring in more men and materials, and for now they still had the benefit of naval support. The beach obstacles and huge concrete shore fortifications (pillboxes, bunkers, gun emplacements and strong points) had not deterred the assault and the 'swimming' tanks and other modified specialist assault vehicles had proved their worth; the Germans had defended well, and were continuing to do so. Some snipers and by-passed pockets of resistance were still holding out in places.

The Germans had been surprised by the Allied landing at Normandy, and significantly still continued to believe this was a diversion for a still-to-be-executed main effort at the Pas-de-Calais. They had been convinced by the 'dummy D-Day' deception plan that the phantom army was poised to strike across the English Channel from Dover, and continued to keep their very real and very strong 15th Army in situ to fight the fake 'FUSAG' formation.

However, a united bridgehead that successfully linked together the five beachheads was not achieved, and the penetration inland was not as far as hoped and certain key cities had not been captured (Bayeux, Caen, Carentan and Saint-Lô). Notwithstanding the non-achievement of these, perhaps ambitious objectives, the Allies had done well. There was still a great deal of intense and bloody fighting ahead as they headed into *bocage* countryside, ideal for wily and determined German defenders. Looking to link, consolidate and expand the beachheads, and necessarily advance further into Nazi-occupied France, meant Allied soldiers had to attack in terrain highly suited to defence in the hands of an enemy with still considerable resolve left. The Germans used the small fields, high hedgerows, earthen embankments and sunken roads to mount a skilful, brutal and dedicated defence. These long since established man-made features were ideal sniper and anti-tank territory and the stone villages highly suitable strong points. German resistance was to be fierce.

The landing beaches having been taken, the fighting for the Bridgehead was ongoing and now the battle within a battle was the fight for the lives of the D-Day wounded. The Medical Aid Posts (MAPs) not too far behind the *bocage* battle front line were the spearhead for this fight, at the forefront of which was Dublin doctor Captain Gordon Spencer Sheill. He was in charge of the Regimental Aid Post at Haute Longueville (8–10 June), where in difficult conditions and without any regard for his own safety he attended to Allied and German wounded alike, even under intense artillery and mortar bombardment, for which action he was awarded the Military Cross. He was later killed along with another Irish doctor, Captain Patrick O'Flynn, at the Rhine Crossing on 25 March 1945, an event second only in combat bloodiness – for the Irish anyway – to the D-Day landings. Nearly fifty Irishmen died in this operation (fifty in British uniform alone died on D-Day).

One of the first Irish doctors to land in Normandy was Hayter Wells, from Dublin, a married man with a pregnant wife at home. He was a veteran of Dunkirk, North Africa, El Alamein and the Italian campaign, but he was not to be a veteran of Normandy because he was also the first Irish doctor to be killed.

Mary Morris, formerly Mulry, from Caltra, County Galway (whose brother Michael emigrated to the US, fought with the US forces on D-Day and went on to enter and liberate Buchenwald concentration camp in Germany) was in the Queen Alexandra's Imperial Military Nursing Service Reserve (QAs) and her diary, held in the Imperial War Museum (published in 2014 as *A Very Private Diary: A Nurse in Wartime*, edited by Carol Acton), tells of how on 18 June, twelve days after D-Day, she was on a hospital ship off the Normandy coast when 'another hospital ship which sailed with them hit a [sea] mine and sank'. An experience familiar to nurses Sister Ellen Teresa Hourigan and Sister Lily McNicholas, of Kiltimagh, County Mayo, when the hospital ship HMHS *Amsterdam* was torpedoed off the Normandy coast. Both gave up their places on the water ambulance and only escaped when the ship capsized, scrambling down the almost horizontal starboard side just before the *Amsterdam* slid below the waves. Both were awarded the OBE.

As the date of the Normandy landings approached, reserve soldiers – including medical staff – were being gathered in Britain. An eighty-strong group of army nurses were among some 1,500 service personnel aboard the SS *Khedive Ismail*, bound for Britain from their station in the Far East. On 10 February 1944, the *Khedive Ismail* was torpedoed by a Japanese submarine and 1,300 souls were lost. Among the dead were eight Irish military nurses:

- Isabella Burrows (25) from Cootehill, County Cavan.
- Getrude Dervan (26), from Loughrea, County Galway.
- Beatrice Dowling (24), from Belfast.
- Muriel Lechy (23), from County Down.
- Catherine Fitzgerald (30), from Douglas, County Cork.
- Maud Johnston (30).
- Maggie Kells (32) and Winnie Kells (23), sisters from Milltown, County Cavan.

Of the thirty Irish nurses killed with the Queen Alexandra's Nursing Corp (16 per cent were from Ireland), twenty-three were from Éire.

From D-Day (6 June 1944) to VE Day (8 May 1945) 850 Irishmen were killed serving in the British Army in the liberation of northwestern Europe.

Almost half of them – well over 400 – were from the twenty-six counties. Nearly 650 Irishmen died in the land battles to free Italy, slightly over half from Éire, and when the European war was over, the Far East awaited. Nearly 300 southern Irishmen died with the British Army in the liberation of Malaya and Burma. There were three days in which Irish fatalities were especially grievous: 17 June 1940, with the loss of the HMT *Lancastria* in the Loire estuary, 6 June 1944, the Normandy landings, and on 23 March 1945 at the Rhine Crossing. Around fifty Irish soldiers were killed in each event. Over 1,400 Irish-born soldiers were killed in 1944, or four a day. From the first landings in Europe (Sicily, July 1943) some 800 Irish soldiers from independent neutral Ireland gave their lives in the freeing of Europe, from the shores of Sicily to the gates of Belsen, and beyond.

After D-Day, it became a race between the Allies and the Germans as to who could more effectively reinforce their positions in Normandy. Those German generals on the ground, von Rundstadt, Dollman and Rommel, had no authority to move reserves. Their air and naval forces answered to separate commands, and Hitler was still convinced that the main invasion had yet to happen in the Pas-de-Calais, so the 15th Army and the Panzer Divisions remained in proximity there. Allied air superiority had bombed the railroads and, together with the activities of the French resistance, considerably hampered German mobility. Allied fighter bombers' repeated attacks on German road convoys added immeasurably to the harassment of troop movements, largely confining them to night-time and making them vulnerable to guerrilla ambush by the Maquis.

Lack of German unity of command, Allied air superiority, the continued German belief in the Allied deception plan and the breaking of the German codes all helped tip the balance in favour of the Allies. These factors, and of course the Mulberry harbours, which greatly facilitated the flow of men and materials into Normandy, meant the battle for the beaches was almost over (Omaha clifftops had still to be cleared), though the battle for the bridgehead continued. In the first few days after D-Day, as early as D+1, 7 June, the 2nd Battalion Royal Ulster Rifles was in action.

Rifleman Jack Allshire, who had landed earlier on Sword Beach, was in a platoon moving along a road that led to Cambes wood when they were ambushed by a squad of Germans dug in behind a ditch. During this firefight some of his platoon were both killed and wounded. After an intense exchange of fire, the Germans were defeated and the platoon continued to advance, but a short time later they came under fire again, and this time Jack's luck ran out when a German bullet hit him in the leg. Managing to make it back to his own lines and to a Medical Aid Post, he was put on a hospital ship to England. Jack survived the war and Jill Kerly, Jack's daughter, applied for the Legion d'Honneur for him while he was still alive. Although his application was accepted, sadly he passed away before it could be presented so Jack's wife, Barbara, accepted it on his behalf in November 2016 in a ceremony at Glasnevin Cemetery

'The Rifles' had been ordered to capture Cambes, a small village in a thickly wooded area approximately six miles from the coast. The 2nd Battalion moved via Le Mesnil with D Company, commanded by Captain John Richard St Leger Aldworth, as vanguard. It was believed that Cambes was lightly held, but as the two woods surrounding it were themselves surrounded by walls some ten feet high, it was not possible to observe the enemy's actual disposition. D Company was ordered to proceed forward and capture Cambes, with the rest of the Battalion closely following in reserve.

At about 1700 hours on 7 June, D Company moved forward supported by one squadron of tanks (East Riding Yeomanry) while the rest of the Battalion halted at the side of the wood. A short diversion was provided as four enemy fighters suddenly appeared and machine-gunned the rear companies, causing no casualties. Here, they met the first French people, who outwardly showed many signs of goodwill. The approach was somewhat costly, owing to enemy snipers on the forward edge and accurate mortar fire dropping onto the Allied troops, but on reaching the wood the Company split: two platoons under the Company commander attacking the village through the side of the wood and the other platoon with the Company headquarters commanded by the Company's second in command, Captain J. Montgomery, attacking through the right edge of the wood. As soon as the Company broke into the wood crossfire from German machine guns opened up, resulting in many casualties. The Company Commander, Captain St Leger Aldworth, was killed on the left and one platoon commander on the right. Lieutenant H. Green was wounded and unable to carry on.

Owing to the high wall and the thickness of the wood, the supporting tanks had not been able to give any effective close support during the attack, and Captain Montgomery, deciding that the opposition was too heavy for his depleted Company to overcome, ordered a withdrawal. The Company withdrew to the Battalion, and the Brigade commander with the Commanding Officer decided that a battalion attack would be far too expensive without much greater artillery support. During D Company's attack the reserve companies had suffered a few casualties from mortar fire, including Captain H.M. Gaffikin, the Carrier Platoon Commander, who was wounded but not evacuated.

The Battalion was ordered to consolidate for the night in positions to the right of the 1st King's Own Scottish Borders (KOSB) in Le Mesnil. The attack had cost D Company dear, its commander and fourteen other ranks killed, one officer and eleven wounded and four other ranks missing, with two stretcher bearers from the Medical Section killed while tending to the wounded. The loss of Captain St Leger Aldworth was a particularly heavy blow. He had commanded D Company for nearly two years, having joined the Battalion as a second lieutenant when it was reformed in Wincanton in June 1940. The son of a famous County Cork family, he had a very fine brain and was a personality of great charm, possessing a brilliant wit. When the 2nd Battalion Royal Ulster Rifles attacked and captured the wood two days later, the body of Captain St Leger Aldworth was found lying at the head of his men, having penetrated deeper into the wood than anyone else. Within a yard or two of him there were a number of SS Stormtroopers lying dead. A fitting end for a brave soldier, but a great loss to the Battalion and the many friends he left behind.

Private Pat Gillen from Galway, 6 Commando, had dug in on high ground at Saulnier Farm near Amfreville guarding the Allied flank, but what they did not know at the time was that the Germans were only 500 yards ahead of them in a green wheat field. They were shelled constantly and had to defend against ground assaults:

We had one very bad day, a counter-attack. In the morning at about 0800 hours – I think it was 10 or 12 June – the Germans put in a very heavy counter-attack. It went on for three hours and was ferocious. We lost a lot, but they lost more. The Germans moved on to 3 Commando or 4 Commando. They got a bit of a belting and they repulsed their attack but it was one of the bloodiest days ever. 45 Royal Marines [Commando] were on our left. At night the Germans always opened up [with artillery fire]. It upset your sleep, which was always very disturbed anyway, so you only dozed occasionally. Casualty figures for our Brigade were very high, 53 per cent were killed or wounded. The dead are buried in Ranville War Cemetery near Ouistreham. We were expecting to stay in that field [at Saulnier Farm] for four days only; we stayed there for forty-two!

Pat Gillen's father Bill had served during the First World War in the British Army with the mounted signals unit of the Royal Engineers. He completed three tours at the Somme and was wounded on three occasions. After France, Pat Gillen was sent to Antwerp, later crossing the rivers Weser and Aller during the advance to Berlin. Pat Gillen retired from the British Army after the war at the rank of sergeant and got a job in the Ford car manufacturing plant in Cork. There he married and raised a family. He joined the 8th Field Artillery (FCA), became its commanding officer and on his retirement handed over the appointment to his son Robin, who in turn has since retired. Paddy Gillen died in 2014 and his son recalls:

My father was the son of a veteran from the 1914–18 war who had served right through from beginning to end with the Royal Engineers [Signals Company Mounted], and was the proud holder of the Mons Star. He had been wounded on three separate occasions. And so I believe that his family history must, in no small way, have influenced my father's decision on his eighteenth year to take off with his three friends to join the British Army on Easter Monday, 1943.

Growing up, I seldom heard my father talk of his wartime involvement. However, I was fully aware, and terribly proud that he had been a member of the elite Army Commando, indeed on one occasion I remember (unknown to my father) bringing all his medals into school to show the guys in my class. At home, a monthly newsletter would arrive from the Commando Association, the newsletter inside an envelope bearing the distinctive green ribbon on its top corner. He would look forward to this monthly delivery, reading of the various commando ceremonies, outings and unit gatherings throughout Britain. Over the years, he kept in contact with his many military friends, a friendship that lasted to the end. Their letters back and forth were always full of humour and high jinks, with always some up to date news on their fellow comrades.

Many years later, when he would speak more of his wartime experience, it would invariably be about something quite funny and light-hearted. I understood that many soldiers have dealt with wartime memories in a similar fashion. Occasionally, he mentioned friends and comrades that were alongside him when they suffered death or were badly wounded, but he would never stay on this subject too long. I can remember the sadness that would suddenly engulf him on occasions when visiting the graves of a friend or comrade. His very good friends from Cork who accompanied him on many of his trips to Normandy [retired Irish Defence Forces Artillery Reserve Officers] would respectively stand back and give him a few moments. He would place his hand on the immaculately kept gravestone and say a private prayer. Often followed by declaring that he must have had the 'luck of the Irish' to have emerged unscathed.

Although German reinforcements were hampered moving forward to Normandy, some inevitably got through to strengthen their defences. Allied air superiority, artillery and ground activity also kept the Germans from acting freely, the difficulty was that those Germans already in place would just not stop fighting. And they were very good at it, helped enormously by the nature of the ground upon which they fought. The *bocage* countryside was favourable to a stubborn resistance by units of German infantry, especially with anti-tank detachments under their command. This combination of German tenacity and *bocage* terrain caused inexperienced, 'green' (new to battle) and jittery Allied 'civilian' soldiers to check their progress in the face of determined and competent battle-hardened Germans defending prepared positions. Nonetheless, by D+4 (10 June) the lodgement area had become joined up into one continuous firmly held front, and any anxiety in this regard, especially about Omaha, had passed. The Battle for the Beaches was over and the Battle for the Bridgehead was going well. Slowly and steadily, ground had been made and the lodgement area was extended. Hard fighting at ground level, naval supporting fire and good work by fighter bomber aircraft was having its influence. That was, until the Allied advance was checked around Caen.

'Monty', General Montgomery, Commander 21 Army Group (Ground Forces Commander Allied Troops Normandy), had a 'master plan' for the land battle in Normandy. Its aim was to stage and conduct operations to draw the main enemy strength onto the front of the Second British Army on the Allies' eastern flank, in order that the Allies might more easily gain territory in the west and make the ultimate breakout on that flank, using the American First Army for the purpose. The plan called not so much for territorial gains by the British on the eastern (right) flank, as for hard fighting to make the Germans commit their reserves, so that the Americans would meet less opposition in their advance to gain vital territory on the western (left) flank. The Battle for Normandy was a battle of attrition, the British and Canadians 'fixing' the Germans in place and forcing them to commit their reserves, especially their tanks, thus allowing the US 1st Army to move south and then east.

Caen, being a vital road and rail centre through which passed the main routes leading to the Allied lodgement area from the east and south east, was immensely strategically important. It was this strategic importance that made its possession vital to the Germans and so aided considerably the fulfilment of Monty's master plan. However, the amount of 'hard fighting' may have been underestimated because the struggle for Caen became fierce and bloody with many casualties resulting on both sides.

There were to be three significant battles for Caen; Operation Epsom (26 June), Operation Charnwood (8 July) and Operation Goodwood (18 July), along with other support and associated operations, before a breakout was fully achieved on 25 August 1944. In the interim the update markings on the various Allied unit headquarters' operational maps were not undergoing any rapid or huge changes, as progress was painfully slow and at great cost to men and materials. That it was not unnecessarily so was always a concern of Montgomery, who was criticised by his detractors for being overly cautious but praised by the soldiers for not being wantonly wasteful with their lives, a lesson Monty had learned during the First World War on the Western Front.

'Fixing' the German resistance into positions and constantly wearing away at their strength and those of the reserves, the various Allied (British and Canadian) operations were actually achieving what was intended. The 'outcomes' were in line with the operational narrative Montgomery had envisaged, but the delayed timelines and uncertainty frustrated many. Meanwhile, on the ground the 'hard fighting' had to be done by the soldiers, one being Major Frederick Crocker, born in Curragh, County Kildare, 1st Royal Norfolk, in an attack on Épron, just north of the city of Caen on 8 July. Major Crocker's Company was in reserve, but were quickly called upon when the attack was held up by stiff German resistance. His Company, with a troop of tanks, clashed with the Germans who were in significant strength on the southern side of the outskirts of La Bijude and the hedgerows surrounding the village. One of the tanks was knocked out and some casualties were sustained.

The attack on Épron was renewed that day and Major Crocker's Company, supported by tanks, was the left-hand Company in the assault. Crocker was to the fore of what turned out to be a successful attack and remained in command of his Company until the objective was achieved, in spite of having been slightly wounded in the face, an action for which Crocker was awarded the Military Cross. His citation read:

> It was because of his outstanding leadership that the objective was gained. Major Crocker throughout directed the whole operation, exposing himself in the forefront under heavy close range sniper and machinegun fire and mortar and artillery fire with complete disregard for his own safety and it was through his actions and devotion to duty that the enemy were driven out of the position later.

The German generals were hamstrung by Hitler, who would not countenance withdrawal of any kind; the German soldiers were to fight and die where they stood. He would not tolerate or allow a 'tactical withdrawal' following the logical, sound, proven tactic of 'retrograde operations' where space is traded for time, to fall back to better prepared positions, all the more able to conduct an effective defence on ground of your choosing, which bestowed tactical advantage.

Allied aerial and artillery bombardments had a brutal physical effect on the Germans, and where this was not actually the case, the psychological impact caused them to become dazed, even demoralised and some practically 'demented'. The Mulberry artificial harbours were effective, but access to the port of Cherbourg was always going to be needed, allowing shipping from the US to dock directly in northern France without having to go to the ports along the southern coast of England and have their cargos unloaded and broken down into manageable quantities for transport by smaller craft. All the more so once the worst gales in forty years wrecked the artificial harbours on 19 June, the American Mulberry not ever coming back into commission again. The supply line is the lifeline of armies, and any interruptions can cause difficulties, even problems to front line troops and their combat effectiveness. This bad weather also hampered vital close air support and aerial bombardments, meaning both sets of commanders had to cope with restrictions and limitations to their freedom of action. However, commanders on both sides readily understood that this was the nature of soldiering. Meanwhile, the soldiers were busy soldiering, while the commanders were busy 'commanding' and for the soldiers, more precisely the Guardsmen of the 2nd Battalion of the Irish Guards, they had to do the 'hard fighting' and at times the 'hard dying' as well.

While there was no partitionism within the Irish Guards, nonetheless even by the start of the war under half of 'the Micks' were Irish and 30 per cent overall from the South. Over 800 Irish Guardsmen were killed in the Second World War, but only 251 – a little over 30 per cent – were Irish, just two thirds of whom were from the Republic. So despite all the myths, the famous 'Micks' were in fact largely British. But other figures are equally surprising, if for different reasons. In almost all other British Army categories, more men and women from the South than from the North were killed. Thus, eight southern Irish chaplains were killed compared to two northerners; fifty men from the South died in the Royal Medical Corps compared to twenty-eight from the North; in the Intelligence Corps there was one Northern death compared to seven from the South; fifty-three men from the South died in the Parachute Regiment compared with thirty-five Northerners. Nearly 500 Irish-born British Army officers were killed and over 70 per cent were from the South. Four Irish brigadiers were killed, all from the South. Thirty-three lieutenant colonels were killed, thirty from the South. Just to complete the general picture of Irish involvement in the war, over 170 Irishmen were killed with the Royal Armoured Corps, over 220 died with the Royal Engineers and some 700 Irishmen died serving with the Royal Artillery. In fact, probably as many Irishmen died with the gunners as with the so-called Irish regiments. Neither in life as in death were the Irish discriminated against, with 26.5 per cent of all Irish soldiers being made NCOs: the figure for the English, fighting for their own country, was 25 per cent.

Enough of the overall, what of the specific, and of the Irish Guards in particular? Well, while taking part in Operation Goodwood east of Cagny, Lieutenant John Gorman, from Omagh, County Tyrone, commissioned into the 2nd Battalion Irish Guards and later becoming part of the 5th Guards Armoured Brigade, Guards Armoured Division, won a Military Cross for disabling a German tank by means of ramming it! The 'War Diary of the Irish Guards', whose function was to give a brief account of events, tells us that:

Orders were received from the Brigade Commander for the Battalion to pass through the 2 Armoured Grenadier Guards, take over Cagny and push on to Vimont. The order of march was No. 2 Squadron, No.1 Squadron, Battalion HQ, No. 3 Squadron. En route Lieutenant A.E. Dorman destroyed a SP7.5 in full retreat. No.1 Squadron then crossed the stream running north from Cagny and moved up the ridge the far side with the objective of crossroads by Frenouville. Lieutenant J. Gorman's Troop on the left literally ran into 3 panzers just over the crest. Lieutenant Gorman rammed one – he was too close and the Panzers too surprised for either to shoot – jumped out and led his crew back to Cagny. Lance Sergeant Harbinson in the following tank was hit as he crossed the Cagny–Emieville road and was badly wounded himself. Of his crew, Lance Corporal Watson and Guardsman Davis were killed and Guardsman Walsh and Guardsman Melville wounded. Of Lieutenant Gorman's crew, Guardsman Agnew and Guardsman Scholes were slightly wounded. Back by the orchard Lieutenant Gorman found Lance Sergeant Workman's 'Firefly' [Sherman tank with powerful 17 pounder anti-tank gun], Lance Sergeant Workman had just been killed, though the tank was intact so Lieutenant Gorman pulled out the body and returned, remounted to the battle. Lieutenant A.E. Dorman had by now reached the ridge and between them they shot up the 2 remaining Panzers.

It appears that the German Panzer tank may well have been one of the formidable Tiger II heavy tanks. Both vehicles were disabled by the collision and both crews immediately abandoned their tanks. There is an alternative version of the tank ramming incident by the Tiger II gunner Hans Thayson to the effect that it was a German anti-tank round 'friendly fire' incident aiming for Gorman's tank that knocked out the Tiger II tank.

Promoted to Captain, John Gorman was later to take part in Operation Market Garden, the unsuccessful military operation to take a series of nine bridges that could have provided an Allied invasion route into Germany (17–25 September 1944). He survived the war and became a member of the Royal Ulster Constabulary (RUC) during the IRA's Border Campaign 1948–52, leaving in the early 1960s to become chief of security for the British Overseas Airways Corporation (BOAC). In later life, he was elected to the Northern Ireland Forum for Political Dialogue in 1996, serving as Chairman 1996–98, and in 1998 he was elected to the Northern Ireland Assembly for North Down and served as Deputy Speaker of the Assembly, resigning in 2002. A Catholic Unionist, he was an Ulster Unionist Party member of the Legislative Assembly (MLA) for North Down 1998–2003. He died in May 2014.

Also involved in the fierce fighting during Operation Goodwood south of Caen was Major Angus McCall MC, from Mullingar, County Westmeath. He was a nephew of Captain Arthur Boyd-Rochfort VC, of Middleton Park House, and Sir Cecil Boyd-Rochfort, racehorse trainer to Queen Elizabeth II during the 1950s and 1960s. Shortly after Operation

Goodwood, Major McCall was invalided back to England with a ruptured hernia, rejoining the Battalion in Germany in April 1945 for the remaining weeks of the war.

Around the same time as Major McCall suffered his ruptured hernia, Guardsman Michael Joseph Quinn (22), from Spanish Point, County Clare, 3rd Battalion Irish Guards, was killed during the liberation of the village of Saint-Charles-de-Percy, roughly 44 km southwest of Caen on 3 August 1944. The hard fighting on the left flank of the Bridgehead drew in the Germans and kept them occupied, allowing the left flank of the Bridgehead to be pushed open by the Americans. This was the strategy and it was working, the bulk of the German armour was kept on the British and Canadian Front, the exchanges between German and British tanks especially proving costly for the British tank crews, among them Irishmen. The Germans called the English Sherman's 'Ronsons' – like the lighter you only had to strike and it went up in flames, an occurrence the British euphemistically termed 'brewed up'. Not always either set alight or badly damaged, the tanks were sometimes repairable and this is where the Light Aid Detachments (LAD) came in.

Robert John Alexander Clements, from Tullyhogue, County Tyrone, joined the British Army in 1940 at the age of sixteen in St Lucia Barracks in Omagh, depot of the Royal Ulster Rifles. Because he had an education he was sent to the Royal Army Service Corps (later to become the Royal Electrical and Mechanical Engineers – REME) and was sent for two years to an Army Apprentice College (AAC) in Chepstow. On 'Passing Out' from the AAC he was posted to a holding unit in Kinnegar, Belfast. He and his colleagues became so bored that when a general call went out for recruits they volunteered to become glider pilots. Fortunately for his family he was rejected on the grounds of being too young, as it turned out glider pilots were not known for their longevity. Eventually he was assigned to the LAD of D Squadron, 2nd Fife and Forfar Yeomanry. At Normandy they were part of the 29th Armoured Brigade, 11th Armoured Division, and equipped with Churchill 'Crocodile' tanks, complete with flamethrowers.

Not in the vanguard on the D-Day beaches, he landed near Cherbourg several days after the initial invasion and progressed through Normandy with the same Regiment, first through the *bocage* countryside supporting the Americans. He described progress as 'depressingly slow' and 'heavy going' as the sabre squadrons laboured their way through the tight lanes and tough hedges. The LAD was kept extraordinarily busy repairing damaged tanks, and when not 'metal bashing' their American M3 half-track was used to ferry German prisoners back to the POW cage. Convincing people to take them was a huge problem. The Regiment went on to take part in notable actions such as Operation Epsom and Goodwood before working its way through the industrial Ruhr. Being REME he wasn't strictly engaged in the hard business of fighting but he was exposed to its gruesome results. Several months later the Fife and Forfars eventually closed in on Flensburg in Schleswig–Holstein, where major hostilities ended.

Another Irishman who was involved in repair work was Joe Walsh, from Athy, County Kildare. On leaving the Irish Army in 1942, Joe Walsh joined the RAF and landed in Normandy in late June 1944 with the 715 Motor Transport and Light Repair Unit. He was keen to go to France to see action, and interviewed in James Durney's, *Far From the Short Grass*, he said: 'The Irish were not worried about the danger. They always went for the most dangerous jobs; tanks, tail gunners and paratroopers – the paras were full of Irish'. He was sent to France and reached there around the time of the Allied 'breakout' from the *bocage* countryside. He recalled, 'We did not see much action. I remember a V-1 rocket landing in a field beside us once though it didn't cause any casualties.'

These Vergeltungswaffe (V, for vengeance) V-1 and V-2 flying bombs, unmanned aircraft loaded with explosives, were directed towards London mostly, timed to fall on the city and its population. These and the newer generation of turbojet engine aircraft, the rocket powered Me 163 Komet and the Messerschmitt Me 262, were being made ready for action. In development also were a new generation tank and a multi-barrelled gun. Hitler was hopeful that these 'wonder weapons' would snatch victory from the jaws of defeat. There were some warnings associated with the 'buzz bombs', or doodlebugs as they were called, in that the sound of its engine ceased, giving some moments' notice before they descended to earth and its 1,800 pound explosive-packed body detonated, causing death and destruction. The first one (of ten fired that day) arrived in London on 10

June 1944, killing six people. Up to 100 per day began arriving in the weeks and months thereafter, and in all it is estimated that about 8,000 V-1s fell on England before the launch sites were overrun by Allied ground troops in September. Among the last to be killed by one of them, tragically, was Captain Guinness, heir to the Guinness Brewing industry dynasty.

Destabilising also was the Allied bombing of known V-1 launch sites. These perpetual air raids on the wider area and on transport, infrastructure and military targets hampered the production and development of other such 'products', like the V-3, a multi-barrelled gun capable of firing huge 300-pound shells across the English Channel at a rate of one every six seconds. This 'London Gun' project never properly got started. Frustrated that bombing alone was an insufficient means to knock out the V-1 launch sites, new 'Tallboy' bombs containing 12,000 lbs of explosives were dropped by the Allies to smash through the reinforced concrete bunkers in which the 'V' rockets were housed, but these were still insufficient to deter their continued launching. So the Americans went bigger again, this time attempting to pack old aircraft full of explosives. Flying them close to the launch sites, the pilots would 'bail out' and the explosive-laden aircraft would be remotely controlled and guided to the launch site targets. The premature explosion of some planes, killing the American pilots along with them, put an end to this initiative, but not before Joseph Kennedy Junior, who was being carefully groomed to be the future Irish-American President of the United States, was among those unfortunate pilots. A graphic illustration of how war destroys potential as well as people, it fell to his younger brother, John F. Kennedy, to become that candidate.

You did not have to be on the front line or on secret missions behind the lines to be in danger. Protecting the supply line at sea off the Normandy coast was 32-year-old Simon Moran from Kilrush, County Clare, on board the 205-foot HMS *Orchis*, a Flower-class corvette built by Harland and Wolff Ltd. When it struck a mine, destroying the bow back to the 4-inch gun, Simon Moran was killed. The damaged ship was declared a total loss and beached on Juno. Simon Moran, a Stoker 1st Class in the Royal Navy, was buried in Plymouth Naval Memorial. On 15 August 1944, just six days before he was killed, the *Orchis* sank the German U-boat U-741 using depth charges in the English Channel, northwest of Le Havre.

John 'Jack' Mahony from County Kerry, 51st (Highland) Regiment, was interviewed in the RTÉ documentary *Witnesses to War*, broadcast in November 2013. He was involved in hard fighting around Caen and spoke of undertaking a night attack where most of the unit's officers and many other ranks were killed, and they also subsequently suffered badly because of daytime shelling and mortar bombardment. He stated, 'on occasion you would be fearful and it was a case, you either fired first or didn't fire at all. You were scared all the time, of course. I was. I saw plenty of good men die.' Later he and a Donegal man were captured, seeing out the rest of the war in a POW camp in Germany.

His obituary in *The Irish Times* in late November 2018 (Jack Mahony died 7 August 2018 at the age of 100) informs us that he had the option of avoiding conscription by returning to Ireland from London, where he was living with his young family, but opted instead to enlist after the Germans dropped a bomb on his house. A native of Laharn, near Faha, outside Killarney, County Kerry, he grew up on a small dairy farm. He immigrated to England in 1936, and after working for a period with a company doing contract work at the Guinness Brewery at Park Royal, he joined the London Metropolitan Police (LMP) in 1938.

At the time, serving with the LMP provided exemption from conscription, but shortly after he and his wife Mary had their first child, Jack Mahony volunteered to join the army following the bombing of their home in Leyton: 'I think there was a need to do what we could … they were hitting me in my own house … I was aware of the risks but thousands of others had done the same. I could see the picture of what was almost certain to happen. It was something I had to do.'

Jack Mahony joined the British Army on 3 December 1942 and, after training in Yorkshire, joined the Royal Armoured Corps as a tank driver. He was subsequently sent to the south of England to replace those injured or killed in the D-Day landings. A few days after D-Day, he was sent to Normandy, where he met a Scottish friend from the LMP on Gold Beach and was assigned to serve with the Scottish Regiment 2nd Seaforth Highlanders, with whom he saw action in France, Belgium and the Netherlands. He first fought with them near Caen, before crossing the Seine at Rouen and liberating Le Havre. Twice wounded, he fought in Belgium and the

Netherlands. When moving to support airborne units near Arnhem, he was captured (along with a Donegal man) by the Germans at Venlo in autumn 1944. He was held in Fallingbostel prisoner of war camp before being moved to Luckenwalde, near Berlin. He escaped when the Russians liberated the camp in April 1945 and cycled to the Elbe, where he encountered American soldiers on the opposite side of the river.

After demobilisation he rejoined the LMP where he had a distinguished career as a detective, including several spells with the 'flying squad' until his retirement in 1973. Jack retired to Ballintotis, near Castlemartyr in County Cork, and in 2015 he was honoured by the French government when they awarded him the Legion d'Honneur for his role in the liberation of France. As the first counsellor at the French Embassy Philippe Ray said, 'Your story Jack, is a testimony to the courage of all men and women who refuse to give up ... in honouring you, we honour the bravery of all Irish men and women who have stood for liberty, equality and fraternity alongside France.'

On sea, on land and in the air also, the war was fought and progressed. Kildare man Michael Coady from Naas served with the RAF in Normandy, in what was known as a close-support squadron; however, he was only there a short time before being recalled to England.

Bomber Command were refocusing their efforts in the face of a still fanatical Nazi regime who gave no indication of any capitulation whatsoever. The Führer had established the *Volkssturm*, a national militia similar to the Home Guard whereby all available men aged between 16 and 60 were liable for duty. Hitler Youth, some aged twelve and younger, supplemented the ranks of an ever-decreasing Reich. Hitler regarded it as everyone's duty to fight; blind, it appeared, to the suffering and sacrifice of his people. General Eisenhower relinquished his first call on Allied aircraft and Operation Thunderclap resumed. Commander-in-chief British Bomber Command targeted the German national will to wage war by directing his resources against German cities and the populations who lived in them. His American equivalent, General Carl Spaatz, targeted German oil installations, believing that was central to winning the war. The full-scale bombing of Germany resumed in September 1944 and it was not long before the effects were being felt by the German people.

At the outbreak of the Second World War, Worth Newenham's father impressed upon him the importance of enlisting in 'a good regiment' but Worth, from Coolmore, Carrigaline, County Cork, insisted on joining the RAF. He trained in Australia and Canada, eventually graduating to piloting Lancaster bombers with 106 Squadron. Between October 1944 and May 1945 he flew thirty missions over Germany and Norway. Worth Newenham survived the war and spent a year with Transport Command in India, before returning to Ireland, where he married and spent the remainder of his life managing the family estate.

On completion of his second year of studying engineering in Trinity College Dublin, Dubliner David Baynham joined the Royal Engineers and was posted to the 27 Airfield Construction Group. The ACG was tasked with building airstrips as far forward as they possibly could so that RAF bombers in particular (with fighter escort) could stay in the air longer over enemy territory, then avail of quick refuelling and enhanced turnaround time. This airfield construction was engaged in all across France, Holland and Germany. Proceeding into northern Germany, he was suddenly informed one day that he had to hand over virtually all of his earth-moving equipment and his men were sent to a medical depot to receive injections. They were sent on an 'operation' to cut enormous trenches in the ground to bury the bodies from Belsen concentration camp: 'I drove around the perimeter [of the camp] and looked down into Belsen; there were still [some bodies] lying in open ground, while others were still being rescued. On the main road outside, there was the Red Cross and a mobile operating theatre.' (Volunteers Project: NUI Cork Interview)

Despite the convenience of these newly constructed airfields, the Allied bomber crews did not have matters all their own way – German fighter aircraft and anti-aircraft batteries firing flak skywards made matters very hazardous. Taking to the skies in large formations of anything up to a thousand bombers brought with it its own perils. The possibility of being shot down loomed large, and continued night time bombing sorties by the RAF had their own associated stresses and strains. There was a high casualty rate among rear and top gunners in the bomber aircraft, in particular. RAF tail gunner Jim Redmond from Dublin, remembers:

> Very often, if the plane was hit you all went down. Most of the damage was done by flak, not fighters. It sounded like a tin roof in a hail storm. People forget it was dark. Things were happening so fast. He [German fighter aircraft] is moving at speed, you are moving at speed; its pitch black, it was a matter of seconds. By the time you picked him up he was almost gone.

Denis Peter Murnane from Dublin, RAF bomb aimer, adds:

> Every time you went out you were taking your life in your hands. If you were to be frightened every time you would never get a flight off the ground. One night, only ten out of twenty-one (in our 4 Group 51 Squadron) bombers and bomber crew came back. You'd be a bit nervous next time. Nerves did get to people. Today we would call it Post Traumatic Distress; then it was called LMF – Lack of Moral Fibre – and you'd be thrown out in disgrace, given ground duties and reduced to the lowest rank possible.

After twenty-one operation flights, his bomber plane was shot down in March 1945. On the ground, having parachuted safely, he was 'captured' by a German Luftwaffe man with perfect English (he had learned it in the internment camp in the Curragh, County Kildare).

The newly established airfields in Normandy permitted a programme of 24-hour flying sorties by the Allies, the RAF by night and the USAF by day. In order to achieve the breakout from the Bridgehead in the *bocage* countryside, Monty's strategy for the Battle of Normandy centred on decisively engaging the Germans with a series of offensive operations along a broad front, but necessarily weighted on the right (eastern) flank. There especially the Germans with their tanks would have to plug any emerging holes in their defence with reserves. Monty in turn committed his reserves on a narrow front in a hard blow: Operation Cobra, the springing of the American troops out of Saint-Lô on 25 July. Based on battle fighting since

1940, Monty's military doctrine (how he fought), rested on unbalancing the enemy while keeping his forces well balanced.

John Joseph 'Sean' Drumm, from Tullamore, County Offaly, was an air gunner in 'Bomber Command' No. 5 Group (1943–5). Prior to that he was in the Irish Air Corps (1939–3). He flew thirty-two operational missions in European theatre, Western and Eastern Fronts. In 1942–3 there was a large exodus from the Irish Air Corps into the RAF.

Michael Quayle (born in County Down, went to school in Ballina, County Mayo and lived in Summerhill, County Meath) was in the RAF Photograph Reconnaissance over France. He remembers the Irish exodus vividly:

> Half of the doctors in the RAF were Irish, same as [for the] dentists and chaplains. In 1942 there were so many Catholics joining up, the Cardinal of Ireland agonised about where to find chaplains and approached Irish Orders appealing to them to provide them. There were the Carmelites, Sacred Heart Missionaries, Jesuits and Franciscans; they were given the honorary title of Squadron Leader. Wherever I went there was an Irishman, the Irish actually ran the Air Force, a tremendous number reached the highest level.

Michael Quayle was recommended for a permanent commission but decided to leave in 1947. (Volunteers Project: NUI Cork Interview)

Monty's strategy worked; the American First Army on the left (western) flank 'broke out' of the Bridgehead going south and then turned east. The fighting in the *bocage* countryside was behind them. The Germans fell back and narrowly avoided utter annihilation at the Falaise Pocket, where the encircling Allies failed to close the gap quickly enough. There was much left to do; a second amphibious invasion of the south coast of France, previously known as Operation Anvil and intended to coincide with Overlord to open up Marseilles as a supply port, was cancelled due to shortages of landing craft. Renamed Operation Dragoon, this was rescheduled and successfully completed on 15 August. The Liberation of Paris followed, with Charles de Gaulle taking a triumphant walk along the Champs-Élysées on the evening of 24 August. The following day, the end of the German occupation of the city was signalled by the tolling of Parisian church bells. That Paris survived intact was due to its German commander, General Dietrich von Choltitz, who courageously disregarded Hitler's express order to make Paris 'a Stalingrad of the west'; to make of it 'a pile of rubble', blow up its many fine architectural splendours and landmarks and burn the rest. President Charles de Gaulle's grandmother was from County Mayo in Ireland and he was a frequent visitor to the west of Ireland, spending time there shortly before his death.

Along with the wartime 'Irish' connection of the Kennedy link with the American presidency and De Gaulle's French presidency, there was another Irish wartime association with a third president. The sixth President of Israel, Chaim Herzog, was Belfast-born and Dublin-reared and educated. His father, Isaac Herzog, was chief rabbi in Ireland and later the first Ashkenazi chief rabbi when Israel gained independence in 1948. As a youth, Chaim Herzog was Ireland's bantamweight boxing champion. On the outbreak of the war, now Palestine-based, he returned to England and enlisted in the British Army, going on to play an important role in Allied military intelligence after the Normandy landings in 1944. He was among those British officers to question the Nazi General Heinrich Himmler, and immediately after the war was Monty's personal representative to a high-level conference on displaced Europeans. Returning to Israel he was tasked to organise a functioning Israeli military intelligence service (1947) and twelve years later, in 1959, further tasked to reform the intelligence service he had created. Going into business, subsequent military municipal-type appointments saw him appointed as Israel's ambassador to the United Nations. He wrote a number of historical books, opened a law practice and entered politics, rising through the ranks, serving in the Knesset (Israel's unicameral parliament) and becoming President in May 1983, holding the office for ten years. He died in April 1997.

With Germany nowhere near capitulation, they chose to fiercely contest the Allied advance into the occupied territories in the Low Countries (including Belgium and Holland) and Germany itself. This of course involved further loss of life and Monty, although now having handed the appointment of commander-in-chief of Allied Land Forces back to Eisenhower, when looking at the short route to Berlin persuaded the Allies to undertake another sudden hard drive into occupied territory to capture and secure bridges as far as Arnhem in order to open up the port of Antwerp. Although already in Allied hands, the Germans still had control of the Scheldt estuary that led from Antwerp to the sea.

Operation Market Garden was devised whereby the largest paratrooper drop of the war (35,000 paratroopers and glider-borne infantry compared to D-Day's 23,000 paratroopers) would capture a series of nine bridges over the Rhine and thus provide an Allied invasion route into Germany. A fascinating operation, and for the most part successful, it followed Monty's doctrine of the 'single punch' against an enemy who was now weakened and staggering about; the deliverance of the 'knock-out blow', as it were. However, the Allies overstretched themselves and went a 'bridge too far', failing to deliver the knock-out they had intended. There were many Irish involved in Arnhem and Market Garden, and the upshot of not totally succeeding was to embolden Hitler to go on the offensive again and attempt one more counter-punch of his own in the forested Ardennes region. Initially catching the Americans by surprise, the German commander called upon the Irish-American General Anthony McAuliffe to surrender at Bastogne, to which he responded using very few words. Only one in fact: 'Nuts!'

A delusional Hitler continued to fight on at huge cost to his people until eventually, and only in the end, with evident defeat staring him in the face, he committed suicide on 30 April 1945 in his bunker underneath the Reich Chancellery building in Berlin. It was an end to Nazism and a successful end to the campaign to liberate Europe, restore freedom and make the world safe again. Yet it came at an enormous human and economic cost. The alternative, to do nothing and let Nazism prevail, was unthinkable and the Irish made their contribution to this worthy effort. It is always important to bear in mind, and act upon the words attributed to the Irish philosopher and writer Edmund Burke: 'The only thing necessary for the triumph of evil is for good men to do nothing.'

13

TELLING THE D-DAY STORY

For some, D-Day represented normal lives that were turned into turmoil, shock and disbelief by events they never thought they would ever encounter. This was especially true of those who landed on one particular beach among the five invasion sites chosen – Omaha. That such a reality existed became evident through the photographs from inside D-Day – from the very 'belly of the beast' – as the great battle unfolded. Blurred, grainy and out of focus, the images were to prove that 'sharp' wasn't everything. They caught real history on the run. Capturing those first moments of arrival onto a fire-saturated beach, the 35 mm 'story telling' lens of one of the two Contax cameras carried by Hungarian-born newspaper and magazine (war) photographer Robert Capa (born Endre Friedmann, 1913–1954) confirmed that it was the tool best suited to show the full horrors of war. Designed to best represent the field of vision of the human eye, wider in the horizontal, narrower in the vertical, it accurately conveyed the message that there are no second takes in war. His being there, in the moment, within the action, revealed the plight of those thrust into a terrible, chaotic, unimaginable situation. The images instantly drew the viewers to the terror and drama of D-Day, to the essence of combat, to the particular predicament of having to fight for one's life. Having first to survive, none of them were really prepared for what happened.

Capa always said, 'If your pictures aren't good enough, you're not close enough', and when his D-Day photographs appeared in *Life* magazine later in June 1944 – the first from the beaches – they were to cause a sensation then and have stood the test of time ever since. Among the legion of photographers who attempted to illustrate D-Day for us, his 'run and gun' photography stands out, because he was as close as an observer could be. In his book, *Slightly Out of Focus*, he describes the moment of his arrival to Omaha:

> The slant of the beach gave us some protection, so long as we lay flat, from the machine-gun and rifle bullets, but the tide pushed us against the barbed wire, where the guns were enjoying open season. I crawled on my stomach over to my friend Larry, the Irish padre of the regiment ... He growled at me, '... If you didn't like it here, why the hell did you come back?' Thus comforted by religion, I took out my second Contax camera and began to shoot without raising my head.

Larry, the Irish Padre to whom Capa made reference, was Father Larry Deery, later referred to by Major General (Retd) Albert H. Smith Jr in a talk on D-Day he gave at the United States Army Armor School, Fort Knox, Kentucky, on 10 April 1985:

> Speaking of Chaplains, the 16th Infantry had about the best Catholic padre there was in the army. When Father Deery spoke, soldiers paid attention, and when he gave absolution on the fantail of our transport [ship, the USS *Samuel Chase*], everyone – Catholic, Protestant, Jew – turned out for the blessing. As far as I could tell there were no atheists aboard.

Later that day, sheltering under a hedgerow, Major General Smith recalls: 'To have survived was good fortune beyond belief. Perhaps, Father Deery's blessing had provided cover when there was none.'

Particularly gripping was Capa's photograph commonly referred to as 'the face in the surf', a soldier tumbling in the tide using a flotation device to keep himself above the waves on his 30-minute approach to the beach. Capa's photograph immortalised the GI (general infantryman) on film. 'The face' is his only image from the assault featuring the countenance of a soldier. Its power, it has been suggested, lay in depicting a single face proceeding towards the beach in spite of the danger. Shortly afterwards, the soldier was shot in the shoulder by a machine gun and Capa and a sergeant helped him to safety. It was years afterwards before 'the face' was recognised as most likely that of Private First Class Huston 'Hu' S. Riley (22) who, years later on becoming identified as 'the face', recounted his inner monologue of meeting Capa on the beach: 'What the hell is this guy doing here? I can't believe it. Here's a cameraman on the shore.' Wounded at Omaha Beach, and later in Aachen at the German border, Huston Riley survived the war and lived on Mercer Island, Washington State, in the house his father built in 1909.

That 'a cameraman was on the shore' was no accident, of course. There were many other photographers on the beaches on D-Day. On Sword Beach was Sergeant Desmond O'Neill, born in Woolwich, London, the son of John O'Neill, an optician. His mother, Catherine, raised both him and his younger sister Patricia after his father died following years of ill health brought about by injuries suffered in the first Battle of the Somme. Educated at St Xavier in Manchester, he left school at seventeen to work for the Manchester *Sunday Express* during the day and for the *Daily Mirror* at night, a grounding that was to serve him well for the rest of his career. In 1943, he was called up for the army and served with the Lancashire Fusiliers. He was then seconded to the newly formed Army Film and Photographic Unit (AFPU) and was one of six still and cine cameramen of No. 5 AFPU, which went ashore with the South Lancashire Regiment, part of the British Army's 3rd Division, at Sword Beach near Ouistreham on D-Day. His cine footage was the first to be shown on *Pathé Movietone News*.

There had been plans to fly the film back by Spitfire fighter aircraft after the capture of Caen, but since it did not fall until July, the film returned instead with O'Neill, who had been wounded in the initial landing. He was later to work for *Soldier* magazine as a staff photographer and then as a freelance society photographer, supplying *Tatler* magazine and others for more than forty years. He married, had three sons and died in May 2003 aged eighty.

Recruited from the ranks of the army, like Des O'Neill, many members of the AFPU had been photographers and cameramen in peacetime. All nonetheless underwent compulsory training in battle photography (still and cine) at Pinewood Film Studios. The photographers had to be selective as they shot their photographs: no images of wounded or dead Allied soldiers, the violence of war is absent from most of the photographs, and there is a focus on auxiliary and support services and British soldiers providing humanitarian care for both injured servicemen and displaced French civilians. Clearly there was an editorial aspect to the photography, minimising the portrayal of Allied casualties and promoting a positive message of the ongoing invasion for the citizens at home.

The irony of the experience, training and storytelling of the British, Canadian and American forces was that their equipment was German, or adapted from German technology. German cameras were better engineered, more efficient and lighter than their Allied counterparts. The Germans, among other innovations, had developed tiny motors built into the handgrip of their cameras. This development, among others, had been done for Hitler's – more specifically Goebbels' – propaganda requirements. August Arnold and Robert Richter established the motion picture camera company, Arri, in Munich in 1917, and in 1937 developed the Arriflex 35 camera with a reflective viewfinder. Captured Arriflex cameras from the front line soon replaced the cumbersome Cunningham C 35 mm combat camera in use by the Allies. The bulk of Allied photo coverage during the Second World War was made with German optics, or at least lenses and cameras that owed much to German photo-mechanical genius. The classic Bell & Howell movie camera replaced the 'Cunningham' camera in Hollywood, and many of the great post-war directors had served in the war.

John Ford, considered one of the greatest Hollywood directors, won four Academy Awards as Best Director (he was a master of filming landscapes, many for Westerns). One of his closest friends was Lord Killanin (Michael Morris) with whom he collaborated on the making of *The Quiet Man*. Born John Martin Aloysius Feeney in Portland, Maine, he was the eleventh and last child of Irish speaking emigrants from Spiddal, County Galway. On 6 June 1944 he commanded a number of film crews on Omaha Beach. The camera crews didn't hold back, and much of the footage was simply too real for the people back home; the government was afraid to show so many casualties on screen. Although Ford claimed to have been among the second wave of troops onto Omaha Beach in an interview in the 1960s, he may not actually have set foot on the beach until a couple of days after the landings.

A book by Mark Harris, *Five Came Back: A Story of Hollywood and the Second World War*, focused on Ford and John Huston (who later took up Irish citizenship) as well as Frank Capra, George Stevens and William Wyler, who were all involved in the war effort. Huston served in the army from 1942 onwards as a captain, making films for the Signal Corps. He made three that were deemed too controversial and so were either not released, censored or banned outright. He nonetheless rose to the rank of major and received the Legion of Merit award for 'courageous work under battle conditions'. He was to live and work in Ireland for a while and had an involvement with the Irish film industry, helping to foster a productive environment for Irish film. He was supported by then Taoiseach Jack Lynch, who through the Film Act of 1970 encouraged foreign production companies with tax breaks if they shot on location in Ireland.

★★★

The story of D-Day, be it through film, photograph or print, has been told many times in many different ways. The book and film of the same name, *The Longest Day (The D-Day Story)*, is one of the earliest narrative accounts of this decisive battle and it is written by an Irishman, Cornelius Ryan, from Dublin. Born in 1920, he was educated at Synge Street Christian Brothers School and chose journalism as a career, joining the *Daily Telegraph* in London in 1940 as a war correspondent.

It was from this perspective that he experienced war first hand and close-up, on US Army Air Force bombing raids, arriving to Normandy post-invasion with General Patton's Third Army, and post-VE Day in the Pacific theatre. In 1947 he moved to America, securing a position with *Time* magazine initially and other publications thereafter. On a visit to Normandy in 1949 he conceived the idea for *The Longest Day* and ten years later it was published, going to the top of the bestseller list and into a Hollywood studio. He was considered an American writer because the US was his domicile country and where he worked, but he was most distinctly Irish and consciously wanted to see true-life Irish D-Day participants reflected in his narrative.

We are introduced to Sergeant James Percival 'Paddy' de Lacy (8th Irish Battalion, King's Regiment) the night before the invasion on a Normandy-bound troop ship, with members of the 3rd Canadian Division holding an amateur night 'with assorted recitations, jigs and reels and choral offerings'. The playing of the 'Rose of Tralee' on the bagpipes was supposed to have aroused so much emotion within Sergeant de Lacy that 'he forgot where he was and stood up and offered a toast to Ireland's Éamon de Valera for "Keepin' us out of the war"'. Later, we meet him immediately prior to landing:

> Some men could hardly wait for the fighting to begin. Two Irish sergeants James Percival 'Paddy' de Lacy ... and his sidekick Paddy McQuaid stood at the ramps of an LST [Landing Ship Troop] and, fortified by good Royal Navy rum, solemnly contemplated the troops. 'De Lacy,' said McQuaid, staring hard at the Englishmen all around them, 'don't you think now that some of these boys seem a wee bit timid?' As the beaches neared, de Lacy called out to his men, 'All right now! Here we go! At the run!' The LST ground to a halt. As the men ran out, McQuaid yelled at the shell-smoked shoreline, 'Come out ye bastards and fight us now!' Then he disappeared under water. An instant later he came up spluttering. 'Oh the evil of it,' he bellowed. 'Tryin' to drown me before I even get up on the beach!'

Sergeant James Percival 'Paddy' de Lacy survived the war and became a travel agent.

Also depicted in both book and film was 82nd Airborne Division Paratrooper Private Bob Murphy (A Company, 505th Parachute Infantry Regiment, 'Pathfinder') as allegedly being one of the first, if not *the* first, identifiable US Soldier to arrive onto French soil:

> To Madame Levrault it looked as if Cherbourg, twenty-seven miles away, was being bombed again. She was glad she lived in quiet little Ste.-Mère-Église this night.

The schoolmistress put on her shoes and a dressing gown and headed through the kitchen and out the back door, bound for the outhouse. In the garden everything was peaceful. ... It was then that she heard a strange fluttering sound from somewhere above her. She looked up. Floating down, heading straight for the garden, was a parachute with something bulky swinging beneath it. For a second the light of the moon was cut off, and at that moment Private Robert M. Murphy of the 82nd Airborne's 505th Regiment, a pathfinder, fell with a thud twenty yards away and tumbled head over heels into the garden.

He too survived the war, going on to become a prominent Boston lawyer, and in fact wrote his own book about his experiences entitled *No Better Place to Die (The Battle for La Fière Bridge)*.

Cornelius Ryan died in November 1974 and was buried in Ridgefield, Connecticut, USA, but not before writing a book about Operation Market Garden. Titled *A Bridge Too Far*, it was published in 1974, the year of his death, and also made its way onto the big screen in the 1977 film of the same name.

Of Irish descent, Audie Murphy was one of the most decorated (Irish) American combat soldiers of the Second World War. After the war he had a successful 21-year career as an actor, unusually playing himself in the 1955 autobiographical film *To Hell and Back*, based on his 1949 memoir of the same name. It was the biggest film hit for Universal Studios at that time. After his death in a plane crash in 1971, he was interred with full military honours at Arlington National Cemetery and his grave is the second most visited grave site after that of (Irish) American President John F. Kennedy. His military career was one of constant involvement in numerous small combat actions where courage and soldiering skills were required and he displayed that he had these in abundance, receiving awards, wounds and promotions, even a field commission. Not involved in D-Day, he was involved in Operation Dragoon, the invasion of southern France (15 August 1944). In all he was involved in forty films, including *The Red Badge of Courage* and *The Unforgiven* directed by John Huston.

The opening sequence of Steven Spielberg's 1998 film *Saving Private Ryan*, depicting the torrid scenes on Omaha Beach, was filmed in Ireland at Ballinesker Beach, Curracloe Strand, in County Wexford. Over 2,500 Irish Army Reserve Defence Forces were recruited to portray the Allied forces storming the beach, a sequence that took two months to film for twenty-eight minutes of screen time. The cinematography was modelled on actual newsreel footage from the era and the modern lenses of the film's cameras were adapted to make them deliver images that looked like cameras from the 1940s. Spielberg and his cinematographer, Janusz Kaminski, also modelled the look of the sequence on the bleached-out grainy appearance of the D-Day photographs shot by Robert Capa. The film's battle scenes were so realistic to some veterans in the audience that the US Department of Veterans Affairs set up a nationwide toll-free hotline for veterans and their family members to call if they felt unsettled by the warfare depicted on screen.

Boyd's War, written by Northern Irishman George Boyd, a Royal Navy Volunteer Reserve fighter, relates his experiences flying a Seafire, the naval version of the Spitfire, over the beaches as a spotter plane for the guns of Allied warships. He also writes of the accuracy of Royal Navy gunners compared to their American counterparts and of being forbidden to engage in strafing 'opportunity' targets, should they present themselves, instead to concentrate on their main objective.

The eyewitness testimony of survivors, research by field historians and examination of archives by academics suggest the story by which victory was achieved. The material has been sifted through, examined, compared for authenticity and accuracy and an 'authoritative' judgement (some aspects perhaps sanitised) arrived at; the official records revealed and the supporting documentation doubled-checked, the history of D-Day has been made known. But has it? The passing of years and the fading of memory all diminish the essence of the truth, the fear and the shock of D-Day. With the impairment of recall, the loss of detail and the development of 'myths', enhancements and colouring of events has left a new generation learning a 'version' from what is assessable − most likely on television, film screens or in books, the substance necessarily telescoped and made cinematic − and the means has unintentionally tempered the trust of the story. A situation arises where Hollywood fiction is taken as fact. There is of course the authors', directors' and photographers' claims of striving for substantive recreation of the look, sound and sense of what D-Day was really like. But can an image ever truly reflect the reality?

Inherent to a book, a film, even a photograph is its narrative, and there is no narrative in conflict, only confusion, fear and uncertainty; often horror and sometimes compassion. The viewer or reader are in the state where the physical circumstances – time and place – are removed from the reality, so there is an automatic insulation and a dramatic difference from the actuality of having been there. There is no exposure to risk, danger or harm; to the possibility of being killed or wounded. The depiction on a screen, a description on a page, a detail in a photograph are that and only that: depictions, descriptions and details of combat. However, the only thing like combat is combat, because it is contested, destructive, hostile, violent and horrible.

There is no glorification in a life ended, to put a finality to someone's existence; a sudden sharp, maybe horrible shortening of a lifespan. Loved ones lost (to us) for ever. The First World War was barely two decades over when the Second World War began. Men would fight in both, and even for those who were barely of age for military service when 1939 came about, accounting for the callowness of youth, any illusionary grandeur of glory in war was not a widely shared or highly held notion, because battle was known not to be benign. And yet the world went to war a second time and millions died, as people knew they would. An evil had to be stopped and there was a moral imperative to act, to force the wrong to cease, to fight for freedom, for our values, for the democracy that others wished to destroy. The Irish men and women that did so deserve our gratitude and respect, so in Ireland, the telling of the D-Day story – the reality of combat – must surely relate the reality of their courage, service and sacrifice. What they did reflected a concern for Ireland, albeit they were fighting in another country's uniform. Neither was this incompatible with patriotism or national identity. Nor were they hostile to the country's neutrality, many believing it was Ireland's best policy at the time.

EPILOGUE

The end of the Second World War in Europe saw the defeat of the mad-minded reach for global dominance by a tyrannical Nazi regime under Adolf Hitler. Freedom and democracy were defended and made safe in the western world by the will, skill and sacrifice of its soldiers, politicians and people. After which a further ideological struggle of value systems resulted in the Cold War between the west and the east, until communism itself also crumbled. After the fall of the Soviet Union many declared a triumph of liberal democracy, and it was seen as an unstoppable force. It was a time when democracies were representative of the will of the people and governance had a largely liberal hue and orientation. In contrast, any existing autocratic regimes were usually those who came to power on the back of a coup or revolution. It was a time when such distinctions were clear and the differences stark, the contrast both sharply obvious and evident. D-Day, 6 June 1944, was the manifestation of a glaring determination of good men and women deciding to stand up for freedom over tyranny; liberal democracy over authoritarianism; and put bluntly, good over evil.

Lately, however, the world is witnessing a blurring of these once highly contrasting, unmistakable and pronounced divisions as liberal democracy is under threat from a potentially 'populist age' becoming a reality. Today, many of the world's autocrats are propelled to office through the ballot box, allowing them to claim they are the legitimate voice of the people while at the same time limiting civil liberties and those hard fought for freedoms. When in power they seek to bring the very infrastructure of democracy under their control and consolidate their hold on office through undermining the notion of separation of powers. In Europe, the trend towards authoritarianism has been fed by populism of the right and left, so often characterised by contempt for the judiciary, mainstream political parties, the media and minorities. In a world that is becoming increasingly interconnected, this 'illiberal democracy' has resulted in a more unstable and volatile world, one seeing different stresses and conflicts than the idea of liberal democracy with its hard-won freedoms and the checks and balances that safeguard them.

The legacy of D-Day was never more important, but it has to be said that some places in Europe are in danger of being undermined, and that which was fought for – which cost so many lives and so much in destruction and opportunities forgone – its liberal democratic values are beginning to become more isolated in the world. Europe needs to remember D-Day, not just for what happened on that momentous day but for the liberating force that it was. We need to remember those many young men and women who gave their lives, sacrificed their futures, faced fear and uncertainty to preserve democracy – 'real' democracy – and it must not be allowed to become eroded from within, its freedoms subverted by power-crazed autocrats, for we have seen what has happened before.

That a D-Day offensive into occupied Europe could ever have been mounted was a tribute to what General Dwight D. Eisenhower, Supreme Commander Allied Expeditionary Force, called 'the fury of an aroused democracy'. The struggle now might not be on the Normandy beaches or through its hinterland of *bocage* countryside, or for the bridges over the Rhine, but within, throughout and on the periphery of a Europe 'occupied' by purveyors of 'illiberal democracies'. A generation ago, a desperate fight wrestled an unfree Europe from the spectre and reality of tyranny, and an honourable legacy of freedom was left to us. Do we now let that which was preserved for us slip through our fingers without again becoming stirred, provoked and aroused; induced to hand on those freedoms to the generation coming behind us? As those who fought on D-Day, Irishmen among them, honoured us, we too must now honour them.

BIBLIOGRAPHY

Ambrose, Stephen E., *D-Day: June 6th 1944 – The Battle for the Normandy Beaches* (London: Simon & Schuster, 1994).

Ambrose, Stephen E., *Pegasus Bridge, D-Day: The Daring British Airborne Raid* (London: Simon & Schuster, 2016).

Barber, Neil, *The Day the Devils Dropped In* (Barnsley: Pen & Sword, 2014).

Beevor, Antony, *D-Day: The Battle for Normandy* (London: Penguin Books, 2012).

Capa, Robert, *Slightly Out of Focus* (Modern Library War, 2001, originally published 1947).

Cawthorne, Nigel, *Fighting Them on the Beaches* (London: Arcturus Publishing, 2010).

Doherty, Richard, *Ireland's Generals in the Second World War* (Dublin: Four Courts Press, 2004).

Eckhertz, Holger, *D-Day Through German Eyes* (DTZ History Publications, 2016).

Farrington, Karen, *Normandy to Berlin: Into the Heart of the Third Reich* (London: Arcturus Publishing, 2005).

Hastings, Max, *Overlord: D-Day and the Battle for Normandy 1944* (London: Macmillan Publishers, 2016).

Mayo, Jonathan, *D-Day: Minute by Minute* (London: Short Books, 2015).

Montgomery, Bernard Law, *The Memoirs of Field-Marshal the Viscount Montgomery of Alamein, K.G.* (London: Collins, 1958).

Neillands, Robin and De Normann, Roderick, *D-Day 1944: Voices from Normandy* (London: Cassell, 2002).

Bibliography

O'Connor, Steven, *Irish Officers in the British Forces, 1922–45* (London: Palgrave Macmillan, 2014).

Parry, Dan, *D-Day 6.6.44: The Dramatic Story of the World's Greatest Invasion* (London: BBC Books, 2004).

Murphy, David, *Franco-Irish Military Connections 1590–1945* (Dublin: Four Courts Press, 2009).

Richardson, Neil, *Dark Times, Decent Men: Stories of Irishmen in World War II* (Dublin: O'Brien, 2002).

Ryan, Cornelius, *The Longest Day: The D-Day Story* (London: Victor Gollancz, 1982).

Ryan, Isadore, *No Way Out: The Irish in Wartime France, 1939–1945* (Dublin: Mercier Press, 2017).

Stagg, James Martin, *Forecast for Overlord, June 6th 1944* (London: Ian Allen, 1971).

Quellien, Jean, *Normandie 44* (Bayeux: OREP Éditions, 2011).

Widders, Robert, *Spitting on a Soldier's Grave* (Leicester: Matador, 2010).

GLOSSARY

Bobbin
: Unrolling a metal mesh to make an improvised 'carpet' to pass over 'soft going' mud or quicksand.

Bridge
: Carrying spans of bridges to enable tanks to mount walls or traverse gaps.

Bulldozer
: Bulldozers protected with heavy metal plates.

Crabs
: Sherman tanks fitted with 'flails' for beating a path through minefields. These were mounted on the vehicles with chains on a revolving drum for minesweeping.

Crocodiles
: Flame-throwing Churchill tanks with a range of 150 yards to burn out the occupants of bunkers.

Fascine
: A bundle of logs bound together and used by tanks to fill in anti-tank ditches or bomb craters.

Firefly
: Sherman tanks armed with a powerful 17-pounder anti-tank gun.

Petard
: Traditionally a small bomb used to blast down a door or to make a hole in a wall. Churchill tanks were fitted with a heavy 'spigot' mortar-type gun for blasting through pillboxes and sea walls.

ABBREVIATIONS

AVRE	Armoured Vehicle Royal Engineers: Specialised obstacle-clearing assault vehicles mounted on modified Churchill tanks with devices for bridging, ditching and blasting pillboxes and sea walls. Sometimes called 'Hobart's Funnies'.
Battalion (Regiment)	Basic Infantry Unit. Comprising of 850 soldiers of all ranks subdivided into companies of 120 each and a support (weapons) company with heavy machine guns, mortars and anti-tank weapons.
Brigade	Military Formation comprising three infantry (or tank) battalions.
CIGS	Chief (Chairman) of the Imperial General Staff.
Corps	A group of Divisions.
COSSAC	Chief of Staff of the Supreme Allied Commander.
DD (Duplex-Drive)	An amphibious 'swimming' tank developed by the British during the Second World War.
Division	The higher formation by which army brigades are commanded and controlled.
DUKW	A six-wheel amphibious truck used to ferry ammunition, supplies and equipment from supply ships offshore to fighting units at the beach.
FUSAG	First United States Army Group: A fictitious force used during Operation Fortitude created

to deceive the Germans about where the Allies would land in France.

D-Day Landing Craft Types

LCT	Landing Craft Tank 236.
LCT	Landing Craft Tank 837.
LCI (L)	Landing Craft Infantry (Large).
LCI (S)	Landing Craft Infantry (Small).
LCP	Landing Craft Personnel.
LCA	Landing Craft Assault.
LCR	Landing Craft Rocket.
LCG	Landing Craft Gun.
LCF	Landing Craft Flak.
LB	Landing Barge.
LBB	Landing Barge Bakery.
LBF	Landing Barge Flak.
NCO	Non-Commissioned Officer (mostly sergeants and corporals).
OB	Oberbefehlshaber (Commander-in-Chief).
OKW	Oberkommando der Wehrmacht, High Command of the German Armed Forces.
OSS	Office of Strategic Services, the American Wartime Foreign Intelligence Service.
PIAT	Projected Infantry Anti-Tank: British hand-held anti-tank weapon.
Regiment	US or German equivalent of a British Brigade.
REME	Royal Electrical and Mechanical Engineers.
SAS	Special Air Service.
SHAEF	Supreme Headquarters Allied Expeditionary Force.
SOE	Special Operations Executive.

SECOND WORLD WAR OPERATIONS

Operation Anvil

Originally planned to occur simultaneously with Operation Overlord in June 1944, this was a second Allied invasion, this time landing on the French Riviera. A shortage of landing craft resulted in its postponement. It was renamed Operation Dragoon and its main aim was to seize the port city of Marseilles, which it succeeded in doing swiftly and with slight casualties on 15 August 1944.

Operation Charnwood

Following the British withdrawal from Hill 112 after suffering heavy casualties during Operation Epsom, Operation Charnwood was a joint Anglo-Canadian offensive intended to at least partially capture the German-occupied city of Caen. The British and Canadians advanced on a broad front and by the evening of the second day had taken Caen up to the Orne and Odon rivers. The Germans retreated from north of the Orne but established another defensive line along two ridges to the south of the city. The Allies maintained the initiative and secured the rest of Caen a week later.

Operation Cobra

An offensive launched by the First United States Army under Lieutenant General Omar Bradley, designed to take advantage of the distraction of the Germans by the British and Canadian attacks around Caen in Operation Goodwood and break through the German defences southwest of Saint-Lô.

Delayed by bad weather, it was further stalled by other hitches. The use of 'carpet bombing' for close ground support for ground troops proved costly as on two occasions they were dropped too close to the troops they were supporting, resulting in two friendly fire incidents. It regained momentum and succeeded in bringing US troops south and west out of Avranches by the end of July 1944.

Operation Comet

A planned airborne operation to use the 1st Airborne Division under Major General Robert Elliott 'Roy' Urquhart to capture and secure a Rhine crossing at the Dutch town of Arnhem, along with other vital canal and river bridges in order to enter the Ruhr, the Third Reich's industrial heartland. Twice postponed due to bad weather, it was eventually cancelled on 10 September 1944 and was replaced by a more ambitious plan: Operation Market Garden.

Operation Dragoon

The rescheduled Operation Anvil, previously postponed because of the lack of landing craft and no great enthusiasm displayed for it by the British. Nonetheless, on 15 August Operation Dragoon proceeded with the US and Free French troops and succeeded in capturing the port of Marseille.

Operation Epsom

In the *bocage* countryside, the British were experiencing a faltering advance. In order to take the high ground around Caen (Hill 112), Operation Epsom sought to first push them south east in a semi-circular axis of advance. Stiff opposition and information received from Bletchley Park, which secretly intercepted German codes, revealed that three German Panzer divisions were advancing towards Hill 112 and this caused the British to discontinue their advance. However, the British retained the initiative and attacked several more times over the following two weeks. Caen was captured in Operation Charnwood in mid-July.

Operation Fortitude

A highly successful ruse to make German commanders believe that an invasion force, the non-existent FUSAG under General Patton, was bound for Pas-de-Calais. The operation achieved its aim to such good affect that even after the Allied landings at Normandy, the German High Command, including Hitler himself, believed they were only a diversion, and that the real main effort would come at Pas-de-Calais.

Operation Goodwood

Led by British Lieutenant General Sir Miles Dempsey, this was an initiative to reach Falaise and terrain more suitable to rapid progress than experienced with the thick hedges, deep ditches and small fields with sunken roadways running throughout Normandy's *bocage* countryside. The operation began on 18 July 1944 and while it advanced the Allied line by some 5 km towards Falaise, it came to a halt when counter-attacked by the Germans and because of a strong summer storm some two days after its commencement. Gains were slight, casualties were high and many tanks were destroyed. What is interesting about this operation is that Monty claimed it was consistent with the agreed Allied strategy of the British keeping the Germans occupied and sucking in their reserves, so that the German line would be more susceptible to the US advance under General Bradley progressing without the hindrance of so many Panzer units.

Operation Jupiter

Launched in the wake of the stalled Operation Epsom, with the capture of Hill 112 as the objective. It was gained, held and lost, changing hands a number of times. Eventually becoming a 'no man's land', each side denying dominance of the Hill to the other. Operation Goodwood followed and eventually the Germans were pushed out of Caen.

Operation Lüttich

A German offensive ordered by Adolf Hitler, to counter the gains made by the First United States Army during Operation Cobra. Although it temporarily halted the US advance, the American forces regained the momentum and the Allies inflicted severe losses on the German troops, destroying most of their tanks and resulting in many of the German troops in Normandy being trapped in the Falaise Pocket.

Operation Market Garden

An enlarged version of Operation Comet, this was an airborne operation to secure the Rhine River crossing at Arnhem along with other vital canal and river bridges leading to it. The concept was to seize and hold these bridges with 'a carpet' of Allied paratroopers while the British XXX (30th) Corps would advance along the route and relieve the paratroopers. Relying heavily on the element of surprise, this was lost with the decision to land the paratroopers at Arnhem, eight miles away from the bridge. Coincidentally, there were also two highly trained SS Panzer divisions there for a refit. Intended as a short cut to end the war, it did not succeed in its objective and was judged to have been a miscalculation or going 'a bridge too far'.

Operation Neptune

This was the naval part of D-Day, assembly and deployment of the vast amphibious armada of over 6,000 vessels that set sail from Channel ports to transport the Allied invasion force to the shores of Normandy.

Operation Overlord

The overall campaign to retake Nazi-occupied northwest Europe. Victory would not be secured until the Germans were defeated and the fall of Berlin achieved. It had a much wider military strategic objective beyond simply gaining a foothold in northern France.

Operation Plunder

An airborne operation begun on 23 March 1945 to parachute four divisions across the River Rhine to establish bridgeheads from which to break out into Germany itself. After five days of fighting this was successfully achieved.

Operation Thunderclap

In an effort to destroy the German capability of continuing the war, an escalation of the wider campaign included the controversial bombing of Dresden in February 1945, the most notorious Allied air raids of the Second World War, which involved 'fire-bombing' or the use of incendiary bombs resulting in fire storms against civilian populations. Prior to this, in August

1944, plans were drawn up for Operation Thunderclap, a massive attack on Berlin that was projected to cause 220,000 casualties with 110,000 killed. The aim was to kill key military personnel, which would shatter German morale, though it was decided that it was unlikely to work and was cancelled.

Operation Torch

Allied landings in North Africa in the wake of Monty's success over Rommel at El Alamein, albeit on a much smaller scale than D-Day. This three-pronged attack at Casablanca, Oran and Algiers was aimed at reducing pressure on Allied forces in Egypt and enabling an invasion of southern Europe.

Operation Totalise

On 8 August 1944 Operation Cobra, the US Offensive to strike southwest out of Saint-Lô towards Avranches, was temporarily halted by the German counter-offensive Operation Lüttich, which was in turn overturned by the Canadians, Poles and British advancing from the north, sufficient to allow the Americans to regain their momentum.

Operation Tractable

An Allied offensive to encircle the German 7th Army and prevent their escape eastwards from Normandy. The Germans became aware of the Allied plans, and knew where withdrawal was likely best achieved. Notwithstanding being perpetually strafed by Allied aircraft, which inflicted much damage and heavy casualties on the retreating Germans, thousands of German troops managed to escape on foot. The town of Chambois in the 'Falaise Pocket' was where the II SS Panzer Corps assisted their fleeing comrades.

Operation Windsor

The Allied advance on Caen was held up at Hill 112 during Operation Epsom (26 June 1944). Operation Windsor was an attempt on 4 July 1944 by the 3rd Canadian Division to assist with this advance, specifically with the capture of the village of Carpiquet, which had a strategically important airfield. The village was taken, but defended by the 12th SS Panzer Division, a two-day assault on the airfield proved only partially successful. The airfield was subsequently captured by the Canadians on 9 July.

Appendix 2
IRELAND'S BRITISH ARMY GENERALS IN THE SECOND WORLD WAR[1]

The three deep water Treaty Ports at Berehaven and Cobh, in County Cork, and Lough Swilly in County Donegal were retained by the United Kingdom in accordance with the Anglo-Irish Treaty of 6 December 1921 over concerns that the U-boat campaign around Irish coasts during the First World War might begin again. As part of the settlement of the Anglo-Irish Trade War in the 1930s, the ports were transferred to Ireland in 1938. Following the outbreak of the Second World War a year later, Churchill asked De Valera for the Irish Ports back. De Valera replied, 'Has Ireland not already given you Montgomery and Alexander?' In fact, Ireland gave the British Army many more military leaders.

Major General Allan Adair commanded the Guards Armoured Division. Crossing with his men to Normandy in 1944, he successfully commanded the Division in the heavy fighting around Caen and Vire in July and August, which prepared the way for the breakout from the bridgehead. He was the sixth Baronet of Ballymena, County Antrim, where his family had been established since the beginning of the seventeenth century, and also had connections in Derry (as colonel of the Grenadiers).

---

1   Source: Richard Doherty, *Ireland's Generals in the Second World War* (Dublin: Four Courts Press, 2004).

Field Marshal Harold Alexander ('Alex'). The Alexander family roots go back several centuries in Ireland. Originally Scottish planters, they settled first in County Donegal then moved to Derry. An ancestor who amassed wealth in India in the later eighteenth century built Caledon Castle in County Tyrone, which became the family seat. Thus Harold Alexander spent his early years at Caledon with summers holidaying in County Donegal. Educated at Harrow, he entered Sandhurst and in 1911 was commissioned to the Irish Guards.

General Sir Claude Auchinleck ('the Auk'). The Gaelic meaning of Auchinleck is 'Field of Flat Stone', a name shared with an Ayrshire village from which the family originated. They first settled in Fermanagh and Tyrone from Scotland during the reign of James I, earning their living from the land or as Church of Ireland clergy. Claude Auchinleck's father John entered the army and on his death Claude went to Wellington College and hence to Sandhurst in 1902. He was commissioned to the Indian Army and saw active service in the First World War and the Middle East.

Field Marshal Sir Alan Francis Brooke. From Colebrooke, County Fermanagh, the Brookes were one of Ulster's best-known families, arriving to Ireland in the Elizabethan era. Granted land in County Donegal, after the 1641 rebellion the family was awarded land in County Fermanagh for defensive services rendered. A Royal Military Academy of Woolwich graduate, he was commissioned into the Royal Artillery. He became chairman of the chiefs of staff, and his firm intercession with Churchill on their behalf was regarded as pivotal at times during the war.

General Sir Miles Christopher Dempsey enjoyed a close relationship with Montgomery. He commanded the British 2nd Army in France on D-Day and during the Battle of Normandy. A descendent of a powerful clan in Offaly and Laois in Ireland, with a very long history, his family was originally O'Dempsey, one of whom built the monastery at Monasterevan in 1179. Terence O'Dempsey, was knighted in the field at Kilternan, County Limerick by Robert Devereux, 2nd Earl of Essex, in May 1589 and later created Viscount Clanmaliere and Baron Philipstown. He was loyal to the Catholic King James II and, as a result, lost all his lands in 1691. Dempsey's branch of the family then left Ireland for Cheshire and are recorded in Liverpool by 1821. In 1945 he married Viola O'Reilly, the youngest daughter of Captain Percy O'Reilly of Coolamber, County Westmeath.

Field Marshal John Greer Dill. Born in Lurgan, County Armagh, he is one of the few non-American servicemen buried in Arlington National Cemetery in Virginia, USA. The son of a bank manager, both his parents died young and he and his sister were cared for by an uncle, the Reverend Joseph Grundy Burton. His early education was at Methodist College, Belfast, then in Cheltenham, Gloucestershire, before entering Sandhurst. He joined the Prince of Wales Leinster Regiment in 1901, and at the end of the Second Boer War was posted to Fermoy, County Cork. After a distinguished career serving in the First World War, he was Churchill's appointee to Washington DC, the vital link in the Anglo-American Alliance from January 1942 until his early death in November 1944. As a diplomat he was one of the architects of the 'special relationship' between the USA and Britain, and he was so highly thought of that the Americans allowed his burial at Arlington.

General Eric Dorman-Smith ('Chink'). Born in Cootehill, County Cavan, in 1895, he was sent to school in England at age twelve and attended Sandhurst in 1912. He was commissioned to the Royal Northumberland Fusiliers in 1914. At the outbreak of the First World War he served in France and Italy, where he was awarded the Military Cross and bar for his actions. In 1921 he was posted back to Ireland as part of the effort to repress the rebellion. He was a brilliant but unorthodox officer and was removed from several command positions. He served well in Africa against Rommel, and General Montgomery later used his strategies to defeat the Germans at the Battle of Alam el Halfa in 1942. Forcibly retired from the army he returned to Ireland and changed his name from Dorman-Smith to O'Gowan, formerly a ruling family in Ulster with connections to his father. During the 1950s he became an IRA officer and would allow his estate at Bellamont Forest to be used as an IRA training ground.

Brigadier Adrian Clements Gore. With family connections in County Donegal and Kildare, he was educated at Eton College and Sandhurst. Commissioned into the Rifle Brigade (The Prince Consort's Own) in 1919, he served with the 2nd Battalion in Ireland during the Irish War of Independence. In 1941 he was selected to command the Green Jackets Officer Cadet Training Unit and during the war commanded the 7th Motor, 2nd Infantry and 61st Infantry Brigades.

Major General Sir Percy Hobart ('Hobo'). His father was from Dublin, his mother from County Tyrone. Attending the Staff College, Camberley, in 1923 he recognised the predominance of tank warfare and volunteered to be transferred to the Royal Tank Corps. In 1934, Hobart became brigadier of the first permanent armoured brigade in Britain. Due to his 'unconventional' ideas about armoured warfare he was retired from the army in 1940 and joined the Home Guard. When Churchill discovered what had happened, Hobart was re-enlisted into the army and put in command of the 79th Armoured Division. His sister, Betty, married Field Marshal Bernard Law Montgomery, who informed General Dwight D. Eisenhower of his need to build specialised tanks. Under Hobart's leadership, the 79th created a range of modified tank designs collectively nicknamed 'Hobart's Funnies', which were used to great effect during the Normandy landings and were credited with helping the Allies get ashore.

Lieutenant General Brian Horrocks' mother was a Moore from County Antrim who met her husband, a doctor in the Army Medical Services, in India. Born in Ranikhet, Horrocks went to school in England and entered Sandhurst in 1912. He served in the First World War, but was wounded in 1914 and captured by the Germans. He was interrogated and held in POW camps, and made several attempts at escape. During the Second World War he led a distinguished career in North Africa, given command of the 9th Armoured Division, and was later sent to Egypt to command the 8th Army's XIII Corps under Montgomery. In 1943, as commander of the X Corps, he was badly wounded during an air raid at Bizerte, and while recovering was replaced as commander by Lieutenant General Sir Richard McCreery. After his recovery, he was sent to France to assume command of the XXX Corps and was involved in the action to trap the German 7th Army and 5th Panzer Army in the Falaise Pocket.

Lieutenant General Walter David Alexander Lentaigne. The eldest son of Justice Benjamin Plunkett Lentaigne of the Burma High Court and educated at the Oratory School, Edgbaston, his family had origins in Navan, County Meath. He joined the British Indian Army as a second lieutenant in the 4th Gurkha Rifles in 1918 and fought in the Third Anglo-Afghan War in 1919. During the Second World War he commanded a battalion during the 1942 Burma Campaign and later commanded the 63rd Indian Infantry Brigade. In 1944, he was appointed commander of the Chindit Force and led the Chindits until it was disbanded in 1945.

General Frederick Joseph Loftus-Tottenham. Born in Naas, County Kildare, in 1898 he was commissioned as a second lieutenant in 1914 in the 2nd King Edward VII's Own Gurkha Rifles and for much of his military career served in the Far East campaign against the Japanese Army.

Field Marshal Bernard Law Montgomery came from a family with strong and long-rooted connections in the northwest of Ireland. The Montgomery's are considered descended from Roger de Montgomerie, a Norman nobleman and army commander from the time of William the Conqueror. This Anglo-Irish family have been associated with Counties Donegal since the seventeenth century and Derry a while later, with New Park House, Moville, County Donegal, coming into their possession through purchase in 1758. The 'Law' in the name further represented this interconnectedness with County Donegal, through a Montgomery marriage there in the eighteenth century. Montgomery is believed to have once described himself as a 'Derryman' to soldiers of the 9th Heavy Anti-Aircraft Regiment at Tripoli in Libya in 1943.

General Richard (Dick) O'Connor. The O'Connor family home was in Ballybrack, County Offaly. Major Maurice O'Connor was serving in India with the Princess Victoria's Royal Irish Fusiliers when Richard was born in Srinagar, Kashmir in August 1889. Major Maurice O'Connor sustained injuries in an accident and retired in 1894, returning to Ireland. On his death the family moved to Scotland, to his mother's (Lillian Morris, daughter of Sir John Morris) home. Educated at Wellington College, he entered Sandhurst and was commissioned into 'The Scottish Rifles' Cameronians Regiment. He commanded the Western Desert Force in the early years of the Second World War but was captured by the Germans in 1941 and spent over two years in an Italian POW camp. He escaped in 1943, and in 1944 commanded the VIII Corps in the Battle of Normandy and later during Operation Market Garden.

General Sir Frederick Alfred Pile ('Tim'). Born in Dublin in 1884, his father, Sir Thomas Devereux Pile, was a Protestant Home Rule supporter. A member of Dublin Corporation, Sir Thomas became lord mayor in 1900. Frederick Pile went to Royal Military Academy Woolwich, where artillery and engineer officers are trained. He became an artillery officer and, in 1939 at the start of the Second World War, he was made general officer commanding-in-chief of Anti-Aircraft Command, controlling the Territorial Army anti-aircraft artillery and searchlight formations and units defending the United Kingdom. He was to command 'Ack-Ack Command' throughout the war and had to cope with learning and mastering anti-aircraft defence techniques. He was noteworthy for defending against the German V-1 'flying bombs' offensive in June 1944, though his plan to shoot into radar-predicted airspace to intercept V-2 rockets was cancelled due to the fear of shells falling on London.

General Nelson Russell was born in Lisburn, County Antrim, in 1897. He was a pupil at Campbell College before entering Sandhurst and was commissioned into the Royal Irish Fusiliers ('the Faughs'). He was to be a commander of the Irish Brigade, which was created in January 1942 following an idea of Churchill's to make the Irish contribution to the war more visible. Churchill also wanted to form a 'Shamrock Wing' (Squadron) in the RAF, though this did not come to fruition. Created in January 1942, the 38th (Irish) Brigade consisted of the 1st Royal Irish Fusiliers, the 6th Royal Inniskilling Fusiliers and the 2nd London Irish Rifles. The Irish Brigade's first commander was Brigadier Morgan O'Donovan, who adopted the traditional clan title of 'the O'Donovan'. He was succeeded by Brigadier Nelson Russell and the 38th Irish Brigade saw action in North Africa and Italy. Suffering from illness, Brigadier Russell was replaced as commander in 1944 by Brigadier Pat Scott of the Royal Irish Fusiliers.

General Pat Scott. With family roots in County Fermanagh, Pat Scott was born into an 'army family'. His father, Lieutenant General Sir Thomas Scott, was an Indian Army officer and Pat Scott was commissioned into the Royal Irish Fusiliers from Sandhurst in 1924. After a spell at Ballykinlar Barracks, County Down, Scott became brigade major of 147 Brigade which was sent to occupy Iceland. Returning to the UK he commanded a battle school in County Down before assuming command of the 1st Battalion, The Royal Irish Fusiliers in August 1942. He took command of the Irish Brigade following the illness of Nelson Russell in February 1944 until its disbandment in autumn 1947.

General Sir Gerald Templer was a senior British Army officer who fought in both world wars. His father, Lieutenant Colonel Walter Francis Templer was from Loughgall, County Armagh, whilst his mother, Mabel Eileen Johnston, was descended from a west of Ireland family. Born in the garrison town of Colchester, Essex in 1898, he was schooled in England and entered Sandhurst in 1915. In 1916 he was commissioned into the Princess Victoria's 3rd Royal Irish Fusiliers. He served on the Western Front during the First World War and between the wars served in Persia, Iraq and Palestine. During the Second World War he served mostly in England, with responsibility for defending the British Isles and in 1943, at his own request, was posted to Algiers. In late 1943 he was promoted to command the 56th (London) Infantry Division. In August 1944 he was wounded and spent the rest of the war on intelligence duties in 21st Army Group HQ, as well as briefly heading the German Directorate of the SOE. Post-war he was military governor of Germany.

General John Ormsby Evelyn ('Joe') Vandeleur was born in Nowshera, India (now Pakistan), though his family was originally from Kilrush, County Clare, where they were the local landlords. Commissioned into the Irish Guards as a second lieutenant in 1924, he served in Sudan and Egypt before the war and led the breakout of XXX Corps during Operation Market Garden as commanding officer of 3rd Battalion, Irish Guards. John Vandeleur's Irish Guards took the bridge over the Maas–Scheldt Canal in the Belgian city of Lommel just south of the Belgian–Dutch border, thereafter known as 'Joe's Bridge', and was described in Cornelius Ryan's *A Bridge Too Far* as, 'the solidly built, ruddy-faced, six-foot commander of the Irish Guards [who] personified the kind of devil-may-care elegance of the Guards officers'.

There were other outstanding and distinguished commanders in the British wartime army with connections to Ireland. Worth noting are those who served during the First World War and, witnessing the terrible loss of life, were determined to avoid sending men into action that could cost so much for so little apparent gain, as had happened in France and Flanders.

- General Sir Richard McCreery.
- Lieutenant General Sir Brian Horrocks.
- Major General Sir Allan Adair.
- Brigadier Adrian Clements Gore.
- General David Downey.
- General 'Joe' Vandeleur.
- General Frederick Joseph Loftus-Tottenham.
- General David Alexander Lentaigne.
- General 'Chink' Dorman-Smith.

Appendix 3
A CHRONOLOGY OF THE SECOND WORLD WAR

1933–1939	After becoming Reich Chancellor in 1933, Hitler consolidates power, anointing himself Führer (supreme leader) in 1934. In the mid-1930s, he begins the secret rearmament of Germany. In 1938, Hitler sends troops to occupy Austria and in 1939 annexes Czechoslovakia. Hitler's open aggression goes unchecked.
August 1939	Hitler and Soviet leader Joseph Stalin sign the German–Soviet Nonaggression Pact, and Hitler puts into motion a long-planned invasion of Poland.
1 September 1939	Germany invades Poland. As Britain and France had guaranteed military support if Poland was attacked by Germany, they deliver Hitler an ultimatum to get out of the country.
3 September 1939	Germany ignores the ultimatum and Britain and France declare war. British troops (the British Expeditionary Force) are ordered to France.
September 1939–May 1940	The months following Britain's declaration of war are referred to as the 'phoney war' because Britain saw no military action.

10 May 1940	Hitler launches his *blitzkrieg* (lightning war) against Holland and Belgium.
26 May–4 June 1940	British and French troops are pushed back to the Normandy coast and are trapped at Dunkirk. A full-scale evacuation, Operation Dynamo, begins. More than 338,000 men were rescued, among them some 140,000 French who would form the nucleus of the Free French Army under General Charles de Gaulle.
Summer 1940	The Battle of Britain commences, the Royal Air Force (RAF) defended Britain against large-scale attacks by Nazi Germany's Air Force, the Luftwaffe. Germany's failure to overwhelm the RAF forced Hitler to postpone and eventually cancel Operation Sea Lion, the planned invasion of England.
July 1941	Operations Sea Lion and Case Green, the planned invasions of England and Ireland, respectively, are postponed by the Germans. Instead Hitler invades Russia.
August 1942	An Allied assault on the German-occupied port of Dieppe lasts less than six hours. Strong German defences and mounting Allied losses force its commanders to call a retreat. The loss of thirty-three landing craft and one destroyer influence preparations for the subsequent North African invasion (Operation Torch).
November 1942	Operation Torch, an Anglo-American invasion of French North Africa commences, aimed at reducing pressure on Allied forces in Egypt and enabling an invasion of southern Europe.
March 1943	Lieutenant General F.E. Morgan appointed Chief of Staff to the Supreme Allied Commander (COSSAC) to begin planning a cross-Channel invasion of Europe.

July 1943	Operation Fortitude devised as a deception plan during the build-up to the 1944 Normandy landings.
	Allied Forces invade Sicily in Operation Husky.
December 1943	General Montgomery reviews the 'COSSAC plan' and throughout early January 1944 revises and expands it.
January 1944	General Eisenhower approves Monty's revised plan and it becomes the SHAEF Plan (five beaches to be invaded instead of three and an extra airborne division to be landed at H-Hour).
3 June 1944	D-Day postponed from 5 to 6 June due to weather information received from Ireland.
5/6 June 1944	Operation Neptune commences, the marshalling and organisation of over 6,000 ships tasked with getting the invasion troops across the English Channel to shore.
6 June 1944	Pre H-Hour airborne landings to secure critical objectives and protecting the flanks of the invasion force on shore against counter-attacks.
6 June 1944	D-Day: Allied Troops land on five Normandy beaches. Surprise is achieved and at the end of the day a lodgement has been successfully achieved. The second front is opened.
8 June 1944	The US First and British Second Armies link up at Port-en-Bessin.
12 June 1944	Utah and Omaha beachheads join up.
13 June 1944	V-1 (Vengeance) rocket offensive against London commences.

18 June 1944	The 'Great Storm' off the Normandy coastline commences and lasts for three days. It destroys two Mulberry harbours; thereafter only the British Mulberry at Arromanches is useable.
22 June 1944	Operation Bagration, the Russian summer offensive, commences, destroying the German Army Group Centre and completely rupturing the German front line.
27 June 1944	Following a combined land and sea bombardment, US Forces take Cherbourg.
29 June 1944	Operation Epsom, southwest of Caen for Hill 112, is unsuccessful.
4 July 1944	The Canadians attempt to take the western approaches to Caen in Operation Windsor. The raid is only partially successful.
8 July 1944	Operation Charnwood, the British attempt to capture Caen, gets underway. A combined British–Canadian offensive seize it two days later.
17 July 1944	Rommel's car is strafed by two Canadian Spitfires from 412 Squadron. He receives a head injury and is hospitalised. It is to be the end of his army career.
18 July 1944	Operation Goodwood east of Caen commences and the US 1st Army takes Saint-Lô.
20 July 1944	An assassination attempt is made against Adolf Hitler inside his Wolf's Lair field headquarters near Rastenburg, East Prussia. He survives.
25 July 1944	Operation Cobra commences, the US 1st Army attempt to spring troops out west of Saint-Lô through the German defences.

30 July 1944	Operation Bluecoat is launched by the British south east of Caumont, to secure the road junction of Vire and the high ground of Mont Pinçon. Operationally, the attack was made to exploit the success of Operation Cobra.
8 August 1944	Canadians launch Operation Totalise, moving southwards towards Falaise; it ends two days later.
14 August 1944	Allies launch Operation Tractable in an attempt to encircle the fleeing Germans in the Falaise Pocket.
15 August 1944	Operation Dragoon (the renamed Operation Anvil) gets underway and the Allies land in the south of France (Marseilles).
21 August 1944	The Falaise Pocket is sealed, with around 50,000 German troops trapped inside.
25 August 1944	The German garrison surrenders the French capital, completing the liberation of Paris.
1 September 1944	General Eisenhower assumes direct command of Allied Ground forces from Montgomery, who is promoted to field marshal.
2 September 1944	The rapid advance in Europe results in supply and fuel resupply difficulties being experienced by the Allies.
10 September 1944	Operation Comet, an Allied plan to land and seize crossing points over the Nederrijn river near Arnhem is cancelled.
17 September 1944	Operation Market Garden is launched to seize a series of bridges that could have provided an Allied invasion route into Germany. The Allies overstretch themselves and the operation grinds to a halt.

23 March 1945	Operation Plunder, a combined air and land military operation to cross the Rhine was launched by the 21st Army Group under Field Marshal Montgomery.
30 April 1945	Adolf Hitler commits suicide by gunshot in his Führerbunker, an air raid shelter located near the Reich Chancellery, in Berlin.
8 May 1945	Following the formal acceptance by the Allies of Nazi Germany's unconditional surrender of its armed forces, VE (Victory in Europe) Day is declared.

INDEX

Index

Index

184

Index

185

Index

Index

Index

Index

Index